the comfort table

the comfort table

BY KATIE LEE JOEL

FOREWORD BY PAULA DEEN

SIMON SPOTLIGHT ENTERTAINMENT

New York London Toronto Sydney

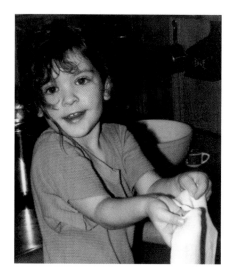

SSE

SIMON SPOTLIGHT ENTERTAINMENT

An imprint of Simon & Schuster

1230 Avenue of the Americas, New York, New York 10020

Grandmother Paul's Red Velvet Cake recipe on page 196 is from *The Lady and Sons Savannah Country Cookbook* by Paula H. Deen, copyright © 1997, 1998 by Paula H. Deen; Introduction copyright © 1998 by John Berendt. Used by permission of Random House, Inc.

Text copyright © 2008 by Katie Lee Joel

Photographs copyright © 2008 by Miki Duisterhof

Wedding photograph on page 205 copyright © 2004 by Terry DeRoy Gruber, Gruber Photographers

Photograph of Paula Deen and Katie Lee Joel on page x copyright © 2007 by Christine Hall

Family photographs on pages iv, xii–xiv, 175, 193, and 242 courtesy of Katie Lee Joel

Designed by Jane Archer

Wardrobe design by Yigal Azrouel

Food and prop styling by Paul Lowe

Manufactured in the United States of America

First Edition 10 9 8 7 6 5 4 3 2

Library of Congress Cataloging-in-Publication Data

Joel, Katie Lee.

The comfort table / by Katie Lee Joel ; foreword by Paula Deen. — 1st ed.

p. cm.

Includes index.

ISBN-13: 978-1-4169-4835-3

ISBN-10: 1-4169-4835-X

1. Cookery (Natural foods). 2. Cookery, American. I. Title.

TX741.J64 2008

641.5'636—dc22

2007049538

In loving memory of
my grandpa

contents

the comfort table is . . .

a place to **see** friends and family . . .

the **sound** of laughter filling the room . . .

the **touch** of a warm embrace . . .

the **smell** of home cooking in the air . . .

and food that **tastes** like love . . .

Everyone is welcome at the Comfort Table.

FOREWORD BY PAULA DEEN

ey y'all, Paula Deen here! I want to tell the story of how I came to meet, and fall in love with, the lovely young woman who wrote this book. Y'all know how much I love tellin' stories, and this story is no exception. For the past few years now, I have attended the South Beach Food & Wine Show in—where else?—South Beach, Miami, Florida. It's always a wonderful time. I love the food, the atmosphere, and I especially love not knowing who I might meet when I get there. Well, at the 2007 Food & Wine Show I had the pleasure of meeting a sweet little Southern girl named Katie Lee Joel. Now, when we met, I didn't know what in the world we would have in common with each other. As is turns out, we have more in common than anyone would ever dream!

Having met briefly in South Beach, Katie told me she and her husband, Billy (yes, *that* Billy Joel) would be boating back to their home in Oyster Bay later that spring. Well, I had to invite them to make a stop at the house 'cause I wanted to get to know this young woman better. Already, I had discovered we both shared a love of food, and she and her beloved husband love spending time on the water, just as much as Michael and I do.

Once they got to Savannah, I asked Katie to be a guest on my show, *Paula's Party*. She was just as happy to be on as I was to have her. After filming, we went back to the house, where we piled on my bed with all my dogs, talking and giggling about anything and everything. We were like a couple of schoolgirls!

Not long after that visit, I had work that sent me to New York. Katie invited me and my assistant, Brandon, to stay at her and Billy's house in Oyster Bay. She said she'd cook dinner, and let me tell y'all, when someone wants to cook for me, I jump at the chance!

Now, y'all may or may not know my view on skinny girls being good cooks. Well, here it is: I don't trust a skinny cook! First of all, how do you know what you're cookin' is good if you don't taste it? And if you taste everything you cook, aren't you just naturally going to gain weight? Seems natural to me. Well, let me tell y'all, Katie is one skinny Southern girl who can cook her butt off! Maybe that's how she's so skinny.

Katie made me a simply wonderful meal of meat loaf and mashed potatoes. Anyone who knows me knows I am a meat and potatoes girl. I love them! I get asked all the time what is my favorite meal, and my answer is always "meat and potatoes." Now, as wonderful as the meal was, I was not at all prepared for the deviled eggs that were served. They were out-of-this-world wonderful! In one short evening, Katie Joel had made me rethink my opinion on skinny cooks. I couldn't think of anything that would make the evening any better until Brandon and Billy decided to get on the piano and play. What a night it turned out to be!

So I was thrilled when Katie decided to write her own cookbook. After spending time with her and tasting some of her delicious food, I just knew that she had made the right decision to share her recipes with others. When I was asked to contribute a recipe of mine, I didn't hesitate to hand over one of my all-time favorites, my Grandmother Paul's Red Velvet Cake (page 196). I hope y'all like it.

I have enjoyed every moment I have spent with this wonderful young woman. She is such a joy to be around and an absolutely wonderful cook. Please let her share her gift with y'all, like she shared it with me. And after trying some of her recipes, y'all are gonna come to the same conclusion I came to, The Lady Can Cook! Until next time, I send y'all love and best dishes from my (and Katie's) kitchen to yours!

INTRODUCTION

People always ask how I became interested in cooking. The truth is, I don't remember. I can't think of a time in my life when I wasn't interested in food. At breakfast, I'm thinking of what I had for dinner the night before; at lunch I'm thinking about what I'm having for dinner. Benjamin Franklin said, "Eat to live, not live to eat." He may have been a smart guy, but in my opinion, he got that one wrong. A piece of my fried chicken might have changed his mind.

When I look back on my childhood, my fondest memories are those surrounding the dinner table. I come from a family of great cooks and big eaters. I grew up in a small town in West Virginia and most of my family lived in our neighborhood or very close by. I had my grandparents down the street, my great-grandmother next door, and my great-aunt and great-uncle one door down. I couldn't get away with anything as a kid!

My family was like its own little sustainable community. My grandpa had an amazing vegetable garden, one of his cousins raised cattle, another raised pigs, and everyone shared. In the summer, we would can vegetables for the winter, stringing green beans until our fingers hurt and staying up into the wee hours until the last jar of tomato sauce was sealed. In the fall, my great-grandmother, Pearl, would gather the apples from our trees and set up a huge iron pot over a fire in the yard to make homemade apple butter. Grandpa would take me to his friend's farm to make old-fashioned molasses; I was fascinated by the process of the horses dragging weights over the sugar cane to extract the sweet liquid that would become that thick, dark amber syrup.

Grandma started teaching me to cook when I was about four. I was young, but she didn't have a choice. I demanded to get in on the action. She would pull a chair over to the counter and I would climb up to help. My favorite thing to make was biscuits—they were just like Play-Doh.

Even though we were of modest means, we ate like kings. I have now dined all over the world in some of the greatest restaurants, but Grandma's kitchen is still my favorite. A few years ago, I asked my grandmother to send me her recipe box so that I could make copies for my own collection. When I opened the package, a thousand memories came flooding back. As I flipped through the cards, I realized each recipe carried with it a different moment of importance in my life—my favorite birthday cake or the broccoli casserole that I always looked forward to at family reunions.

Sometimes that life seems a million miles away. I now live in New York and I married a rock star. Strange, huh? I'm a hillbilly princess. People always think we live in the fast lane, and, sure, sometimes we do. But at heart, we are really just homebodies like everybody else. Being on tour with a rock 'n' roll band may sound glamorous, but after a while, it makes you feel like Willy Loman in *Death of Salesman*. When my husband has been away on tour, he can't wait to get home and have meat loaf. Nothing is more comforting than a home-cooked meal.

I love to entertain at home with my friends, whether it is a small group for a weeknight dinner or twenty people for a cocktail party. The most important thing Grandma taught me about cooking didn't

necessarily have anything to do with food. It had to do with the way you make people feel in your home. They have to feel comfortable. This can be accomplished by thinking ahead: Choose a menu that is easily executed; set the table the night before; have drinks and appetizers ready before guests arrive. Nothing pleases me more than the sound of my guests' laughter. Then I know my job is done.

Comfort food starts at the source. In order for me to be truly comforted by the food I eat, I need to know where it comes from. I call it "conscious consumption"—being aware of what you eat and how it affects not only your body, but ultimately the environment and future generations. I grew up eating locally farmed seasonal foods. These foods tasted better, and they were also healthier for me and the Earth. I encourage you to seek out local farms and organic retailers in your area to eat seasonally.

In this book you will not only find recipes perfect for a weeknight dinner on the run or your next celebration, but also entertaining tips for creating your own "Comfort Table."

These recipes that I am sharing with you are my family heirlooms. My grandmother didn't have jewels to pass down to me, but the secret to her peach cobbler is more precious to me than any diamond or ruby. I hope you enjoy these recipes as much as my family does and entertain with them for years to come.

—KATIE LEE JOEL

TIPS FOR ENTERTAINING

I LOVE every step that goes into planning a party at my home—from designing the menu, to preparing the food, to getting dressed, to welcoming the guests, it's all a pleasure. It wasn't always so easy for me, but after some practice and learning from mistakes, my parties are now fun not only for my guests but for me as well. So many hosts make the mistake of taking on more than they can handle and end up not enjoying themselves. These are my tips for making any party a success.

CHOOSE A DATE. Look at your calendar and pick an open date that is also clear the day before so that you have time to prep.

DECIDE HOW MANY PEOPLE YOU CAN MANAGE. Make a guest list, including contact information for each attendee. For a formal gathering, invite guests with mailed invitations; for a casual occasion, e-mail or phone invites are fine.

DECIDE ON A MENU. Ask yourself some questions: Do any of your guests have dietary limitations? How do you want the food to be served—sit-down, buffet, or family-style? Write the menu with your appetizers, main course, and desserts, and decide what cocktails and wine you would like to serve. Based on your menu, make a grocery list divided into sections of produce, meat/seafood, dairy, pantry, etc., for efficient shopping.

SET THE TABLE THE NIGHT BEFORE. Get creative with the table's décor; try using flowers, fruit, or objects that go with the theme of the party. I always use unscented candles on the table to create ambience. Also, set out all of the serving dishes and utensils you plan to use. This way, if you are missing something, you will have time to get it before the party.

CREATE A PLAYLIST. Select songs that enhance the mood you are looking to create, and make a playlist for your iPod. I like something upbeat for cocktails and mellow for dinner. Be sure that the volume isn't too loud—nobody should feel the need to shout over dinner.

PROPERLY EQUIP YOUR GUEST BATHROOM. Put out fresh hand towels, soap, a scented candle, plenty of toilet tissue, and a small flower arrangement. (A discreetly placed plunger will help avoid any embarrassing situations!)

DESIGNATE AN HOUR TO GET YOURSELF PARTY-READY. Choose an outfit that makes you feel stylish, yet that is still comfortable enough to work in the kitchen. I usually avoid light colors to prevent any obvious stains if something splashes on me while cooking.

HAVE DRINKS AND HORS D'OEUVRES READY FOR YOUR GUESTS' ARRIVAL. I like to hand my guests a drink as soon as they walk in the door to get the festivities started.

IF SOMETHING GOES NOT ACCORDING TO PLAN, DON'T ANNOUNCE IT. Your guests will most likely never know the difference if you don't tell them.

RELAX! As the host, you set the tone for the party. If you are frazzled, your guests will feel it. Guests should feel comfortable and welcome at all times.

MOST IMPORTANT, HAVE FUN! It *is* a party, for crying out loud!

STARTERS

Before dinner in the summertime, my grandmother would always serve a plate of fresh vegetables from my grandfather's garden. It would usually consist of sliced tomatoes, cucumbers, and scallions with a sprinkling of salt and pepper. I looked forward to her simple crudités every evening.

The hors d'oeuvres really set the tone for the meal. Consider the main course when choosing what to serve as a starter. Don't make anything too rich if the entree is especially heavy. If you are having a cocktail party, make bite-size portions to keep foods easy to eat.

HOT SPINACH AND ARTICHOKE DIP

Whenever my mom had dinner parties, she would employ me as her "caterer." My hot spinach and artichoke dip was always on the menu, and her regular guests have come to expect it on every occasion. It is fantastic for entertaining because it can be assembled ahead of time and then baked just before your guests arrive.

One 8-ounce package cream cheese, at room temperature

One 9-ounce package frozen artichoke hearts (drained jarred or canned, cooked fresh, or frozen, but not marinated)

1 cup steamed spinach (1 pound raw or one 10-ounce package frozen chopped spinach, thawed), well drained

½ cup mayonnaise

½ cup grated Parmesan cheese

2 garlic cloves

6 large fresh basil leaves

½ teaspoon kosher salt

¼ teaspoon freshly ground black pepper

¼ cup shredded mozzarella cheese

Preheat the oven to 375° F. Grease a 2-quart baking dish.
In a food processor, combine the cream cheese, artichoke hearts, spinach, mayo, Parmesan, garlic, basil, salt, and pepper. Spoon into the baking dish. Top with the mozzarella. Bake until bubbling and the top is golden brown, 25 to 30 minutes.

Serve with crackers, tortilla chips, or toasted rustic bread.

YIELD: 4 SERVINGS
PREP TIME: 10 MINUTES
COOK TIME: 30 MINUTES

GUACAMOLE

I am a guacamole fanatic. When I make it for parties, I usually have to make two batches because I am sure to finish off most of it before it's serving time.

In a food processor, pulse the garlic and serrano pepper until finely chopped. Add the avocados, lime juice, salt, and pepper and blend to the desired consistency. Add cilantro and pulse until combined. Transfer to a serving bowl. Stir in the tomato by hand.

Serve with tortilla chips.

YIELD: 3 CUPS
PREP TIME: 15 MINUTES

4 garlic cloves

½ to 1 serrano pepper, stemmed (depending on desired spiciness)

4 Haas avocados, halved, pitted, and peeled

Juice of 1 lime

1½ teaspoons kosher salt

1 teaspoon freshly ground black pepper

½ cup chopped fresh cilantro

1 tomato, diced

FRIED GREEN TOMATOES

I am a pretty patient person, but not when it comes to my tomato plants. I'm constantly monitoring their growth and anxiously waiting for their flesh to redden. Luckily, I have this recipe to whet my appetite. I love to eat fried green tomatoes with rémoulade, but I also love them on a classic BLT.

For the fried green tomatoes

1 cup cornmeal

1 cup all-purpose flour

1½ teaspoons onion powder

1½ teaspoons garlic powder

½ teaspoon kosher salt

½ teaspoon freshly ground black pepper

Pinch of cayenne pepper

1 cup buttermilk

½ cup vegetable oil

4 large green tomatoes (like beefsteak, Big Boy, or Celebrity), sliced ½-inch thick

Rémoulade (recipe follows)

For the rémoulade

1 cup mayonnaise

3 tablespoons ketchup

1 scallion, thinly sliced (about 2 tablespoons)

1 tablespoon apple cider vinegar

1½ teaspoons dry mustard (like Coleman's)

1 teaspoon hot sauce (like Tabasco), or to taste

½ teaspoon kosher salt

¼ teaspoon freshly ground black pepper

FOR THE FRIED GREEN TOMATOES

In a medium shallow bowl, mix the cornmeal, flour, onion powder, garlic powder, salt, pepper, and cayenne. Fill a small shallow bowl with buttermilk. Place the bowls next to each other and next to the stove.

Heat the oil in a large heavy skillet (preferably cast-iron) over medium-high heat. The oil should be hot but not smoking.

Dip the tomatoes in the buttermilk and dredge in the cornmeal mixture. Fry the tomatoes, in batches if necessary, until the crust is golden brown and crunchy, 4 to 5 minutes on each side. Drain on paper towels. Transfer the tomatoes to a serving plate and dollop with rémoulade or pass the rémoulade alongside.

YIELD: 4 TO 6 SERVINGS
PREP TIME: 15 MINUTES
COOK TIME: 10 TO 20 MINUTES

FOR THE RÉMOULADE

Mix the mayo, ketchup, scallion, vinegar, mustard, hot sauce, salt, and pepper in a small bowl. Transfer to a serving bowl. Extra rémoulade can be saved in the refrigerator in an airtight container for up to one week.

YIELD: 1 ¼ CUPS
PREP TIME: 5 MINUTES

DEVILED EGGS

I specifically remember the first time I made deviled eggs. I was twelve years old and trying to impress my friend with my culinary skills. I had no idea how to make them, but somehow I managed to whip them up—they have been one of my specialties ever since. The first time I made dinner for my good friend Paula Deen, I served her these and she told me they were the best deviled eggs she'd ever eaten. Quite a compliment!

Place the eggs in a large saucepan and cover with water. Add the vinegar. Bring to a boil over high heat. Turn off the heat and cover. Let sit for 15 to 18 minutes. Drain off the water. When cool enough to touch, remove shells.

Slice each egg in half lengthwise. Remove the yolks and place in a food processor. Arrange the whites on a serving platter. Add the mayo, mustard, salt, and pepper to the yolks. Blend until smooth. Scoop the yolk mixture into a resealable plastic bag. Use scissors to snip off a bottom corner of the bag. Use the bag like a pastry bag to pipe the yolk mixture into the egg whites. Sprinkle each deviled egg half with paprika. Cover loosely and chill until serving time.

YIELD: 6 TO 8 SERVINGS
PREP TIME: 10 MINUTES
INACTIVE PREP TIME: 15 MINUTES
COOK TIME: 15 TO 18 MINUTES

1 dozen large eggs

2 tablespoons white vinegar

1 cup mayonnaise

1 tablespoon yellow prepared mustard

¼ teaspoon kosher salt

¼ teaspoon freshly ground black pepper

Paprika

GORGONZOLA AND FIG CROSTINI

The creamy texture and salty flavor of the Gorgonzola cheese paired with the sweet, earthy flavor of the fig jam makes these crostini a little bite of heaven. You can always find Gorgonzola cheese and fig jam in my refrigerator, so these are my go-to snack for unexpected guests. They pair perfectly with a glass of red wine.

1 loaf French bread, cut into about 32 ½-inch slices

2 to 3 tablespoons olive oil

½ pound Gorgonzola dolce, room temperature

¾ cup fig jam

Preheat the oven to 350° F.

Place the bread in one layer on one or two baking sheets. Drizzle or brush the bread with the olive oil. Bake for 10 to 12 minutes, until crisp and golden. Remove from the oven and let cool slightly.

Spread each slice of toast with about 1 tablespoon Gorgonzola. Top with a teaspoon-size dollop of fig jam. Transfer to a serving platter.

YIELD: 6 TO 8 SERVINGS
PREP TIME: 10 MINUTES
COOK TIME: 10 MINUTES

HUMMUS WITH HERBED PITA CRISPS

I always keep hummus in my refrigerator for snacking. I love to use it as a dip for vegetables or a spread on a sandwich. When I have guests for dinner, I serve it with these homemade herbed pita crisps. The pitas don't take any time to make, but they make your guests think that you did something really special.

For the pita crisps

4 tablespoons (½ stick) unsalted butter, at room temperature

3 tablespoons minced fresh herbs (chives, parsley, rosemary, thyme, cilantro, etc.)

4 pitas, split in half and each half cut into fourths (I like to use whole wheat for a "nuttier" flavor)

Kosher salt

For the hummus

Two 15-ounce cans chickpeas, drained, juice reserved

2 garlic cloves

¼ cup fresh lemon juice

¼ cup tahini

1 teaspoon ground cumin

½ cup extra virgin olive oil

1 teaspoon kosher salt

FOR THE PITA CRISPS

Preheat the oven to 400° F. In a mini food processor, combine the butter and herbs and pulse until well combined. Spread the herb butter onto the pita slices. Sprinkle with salt and bake until crisp, about 10 minutes.

FOR THE HUMMUS

In a food processor, combine the chickpeas, garlic, lemon juice, tahini, and cumin. Pulse until smooth. With the food processor running, add the olive oil in a steady stream. Season with the salt and puree until very smooth. If the mixture is too thick, add 2 tablespoons of the reserved chickpea juice at a time until the desired consistency is reached.

YIELD: 4 TO 6 SERVINGS
PREP TIME: 20 MINUTES
COOK TIME: 10 MINUTES

PIMENTO CHEESE SPREAD

My grandfather used to make the best pimento cheese spread. He didn't have a food processor, so he made it with an old-fashioned meat grinder. He used Velveeta, which gave the spread a really mild flavor. In my recipe, I use sharp Cheddar for a little extra bite, but you can substitute just about any hard cheese, like Gouda or fontina. When I would come home from college, he would always send me back to school with some. I love it spread on crackers or as finger sandwiches on white bread.

In a food processor, pulse the cheese until it looks like fine meal. Add the mayo and blend until creamy. Add the pimentos, relish, onion powder, salt, pepper, and hot sauce. Blend until combined.

Serve with crackers or toasted bread.

YIELD: 2 CUPS
PREP TIME: 15 MINUTES

4 cups shredded sharp Cheddar cheese

½ cup mayonnaise

¼ cup pimentos, whole or chopped, drained

1 tablespoon pickle relish

1 teaspoon onion powder

½ teaspoon kosher salt

¼ teaspoon freshly ground black pepper

Dash of hot sauce, optional (use as much or as little as you like)

ASIAN-STYLE TUNA MEATBALLS WITH MANGO CHUTNEY

Grinding fresh tuna steaks in a food processor gives the meaty fish a consistency similar to ground beef. I often make tuna burgers this way, so I decided to try making "meatballs." The method works great and is a terrific alternative to its traditional meat counterpart.

For the tuna meatballs

1 pound fresh tuna steak, cut into 3-inch cubes

½ cup bread crumbs

1 large egg

¼ cup grated yellow onion, excess water squeezed out (about ⅓ medium onion)

¼ cup minced fresh cilantro

1 tablespoon soy sauce

1 teaspoon grated ginger (from a 1-inch knob)

1 teaspoon sesame oil

½ cup lightly toasted sesame seeds

For the dipping sauce

1 cup mango chutney

¼ cup roughly chopped fresh cilantro

FOR THE TUNA MEATBALLS

Preheat oven to 500° F. Line a baking sheet with parchment paper.

Place a few pieces of the tuna in a food processor and pulse for a couple of seconds, until it has the consistency of ground meat. Set the chopped tuna aside in a large bowl. Continue with the remaining tuna.

Add the bread crumbs, egg, onion, cilantro, soy sauce, ginger, and sesame seeds to the ground tuna and mix well with your hands. Shape into about twenty-four 1½-inch diameter balls.

Spread the sesame seeds in a shallow dish. Roll the tuna meatballs in the sesame seeds to coat lightly. Place on the baking sheet and bake for 7 minutes, until well done.

FOR THE DIPPING SAUCE

Meanwhile, combine the mango chutney and cilantro in a food processor and pulse until smooth. Transfer to a serving bowl.

Place the meatballs on a serving platter and serve with the dipping sauce alongside.

YIELD: 4 TO 6 SERVINGS
PREP TIME: 25 MINUTES
COOK TIME: 7 MINUTES

FIESTA WONTONS

Believe it or not, this recipe started out as Italian meatballs. I was in my kitchen writing recipes, and I wanted to make meatballs. Somehow the recipe evolved into Mexican-inspired meat wrapped in a wonton, deep-fried, and served with a side of salsa. They are like little fried tacos.

In a medium bowl, combine the beef, onion, cream cheese, Cheddar, the whole egg, bread crumbs, taco seasoning, and cilantro.

Line a baking sheet with parchment paper. Place the wonton squares on a dry work surface. Place 1 mounded teaspoon of the meat mixture in the middle of each wonton. Brush the wonton's edges with egg white using a pastry brush and fold to seal in a triangle. Place the wontons on the baking sheet. Cover with plastic wrap and refrigerate for 20 minutes.

In a deep heavy pot, heat the canola oil to 375° F. A few at a time fry the wontons until golden brown, about 1 minute per side. Remove with a slotted spoon and drain on paper towels.

Garnish with fresh cilantro leaves and serve immediately with salsa.

For a reduced-fat version: Instead of frying, preheat the oven to 500° F. Brush the wontons with lightly beaten egg white and bake for 7 to 8 minutes.

YIELD: ABOUT 36 WONTONS (6 SERVINGS)
PREP TIME: 30 MINUTES
COOK TIME: 10 MINUTES

½ pound lean ground beef

¼ cup grated yellow onion

2 ounces cream cheese (¼ cup), at room temperature

¼ cup shredded Cheddar cheese

1 large whole egg

2 tablespoons dry bread crumbs

2 tablespoons taco seasoning

2 tablespoons minced fresh cilantro

36 square wonton wrappers

1 large egg white, lightly beaten

2 cups canola oil

Fresh cilantro leaves

Salsa

ORANGE-ONION MARMALADE AND GOAT CHEESE CANAPÉS

Caramelizing onions brings out all of their sweet flavor, and adding orange marmalade and honey takes it to another level. I usually make the onion marmalade ahead of time and assemble the canapés before my guests arrive.

One 1-pound loaf very thinly sliced white bread (like Pepperidge Farm)

2 tablespoons olive oil

2 medium yellow onions, sliced into thin rings

¼ cup orange marmalade

1 tablespoon honey

2 tablespoons red wine vinegar

1/2 teaspoon kosher salt

1/4 teaspoon freshly ground black pepper

5 ounces soft goat cheese

2 ounces cream cheese (¼ cup)

1 tablespoon fresh thyme leaves

¼ teaspoon garlic powder

Minced fresh parsley

Preheat the oven to 500° F.

Use a biscuit cutter or a juice glass to cut each piece of bread into rounds 2 to 2½ inches in diameter. Place in one layer on an ungreased baking sheet and bake for about 3 minutes, until lightly toasted. Remove from the oven and set aside.

Heat the olive oil in a medium skillet over medium heat. Add the onions and sauté 5 minutes. Add 2 tablespoons water and reduce heat to medium-low. Cook, stirring occasionally, for about 20 minutes, until the onions are a caramel color and reduced in size. Stir in the marmalade, honey, vinegar, salt, and pepper. Simmer until most of the liquid has evaporated, 5 to 7 minutes more. Remove from the heat.

Meanwhile, in a food processor, combine the cream cheese, goat cheese, thyme, and garlic powder. Pulse until evenly mixed and creamy.

Evenly spread each toast with cheese and top with onions. Garnish with parsley and serve.

YIELD: 6 TO 8 SERVINGS
PREP TIME: 20 MINUTES
COOK TIME: 35 MINUTES

VIRGIN BLOODY MARY ASPIC

Aspics are a Southern classic. A couple of years ago, I was eating at Alain Ducasse in Paris and was surprised when tomato aspic was presented as the *amuse bouche*. Was I in France or back in West Virginia? On a hot summer day, this tomato aspic is so refreshing. You can make it in a loaf pan and serve it sliced on a bed of greens, or for a more special presentation, make it in a ring mold and fill the center with my Lobster Salad (page 47).

Lightly oil a 9 by 5 by 3-inch loaf pan.

Working in batches if necessary, puree the tomatoes, tomato juice, Worcestershire, lemon juice, onion and garlic powders, celery seed, pepper, and salt in a blender. Pour into a medium saucepan. Bring to a boil. Remove 1 cup and mix in the gelatin. Let sit for five minutes, until the gelatin is dissolved. Add back to the rest of the tomato mixture and stir until combined. Pour into the mold. Chill at least 6 hours.

YIELD: 6 SERVINGS
PREP TIME: 15 MINUTES
INACTIVE PREP TIME: 6 HOURS
COOK TIME: 10 MINUTES

1½ pounds ripe tomatoes, seeded, or one 28-ounce can whole tomatoes, with juice

2 cups tomato juice

1 tablespoon Worcestershire sauce

2 tablespoons fresh lemon juice

1 teaspoon onion powder

1 teaspoon garlic powder

1 teaspoon celery seed

1 teaspoon freshly ground black pepper

2 teaspoons kosher salt

Three ¼-ounce packets unflavored gelatin

CHORIZO GRITS CAKES WITH CILANTRO CREAM

I absolutely love grits because they are so versatile. Basically the same as polenta, only coarser, grits can be mixed with just about anything and will taste good. This recipe is incredibly easy, so be creative and try substituting different cheeses, meats, or seasonings. I have these for breakfast with eggs, but they also make great hors d'oeuvres at a party. I made 1,500 grits cakes at the South Beach Wine & Food Festival. Instead of chorizo, I used rock shrimp and added a tablespoon of chopped chipotle peppers.

For the chorizo grits cakes

½ cup diced chorizo, cut in small pieces

3 cups chicken broth

3 cups milk

1 teaspoon kosher salt

1/8 teaspoon saffron threads

2 cups regular grits (not instant or quick-cooking)

½ cup grated Cheddar cheese

1 tablespoon unsalted butter

½ teaspoon freshly ground black pepper

3 tablespoons olive oil

For the cilantro cream

¾ cup sour cream

½ cup loosely packed fresh cilantro leaves

Pinch of kosher salt

Pinch of freshly ground black pepper

Special Equipment: 2½-inch biscuit cutter

FOR THE CHORIZO GRITS CAKES

In a small skillet over medium heat, cook the chorizo until the fat is rendered. Set aside to drain on paper towels.

In a large saucepan over medium-high heat, combine the chicken stock, milk, and salt, and bring to a gentle boil. Stir in the saffron threads until dissolved, about 2 minutes. Slowly whisk in grits and reduce the heat to a very low simmer, stirring occasionally to keep the grits from scorching. Cook, stirring frequently until the liquid has been absorbed and the grits are thick, about 30 minutes. Stir in the reserved chorizo, cheese, butter, and pepper.

Grease a 13 by 9-inch baking dish. Pour in the grits and smooth out into an even layer. Let cool completely. Cover with plastic wrap and refrigerate for 2 hours, or up to overnight.

Use a 2½-inch biscuit cutter to cut out 15 cakes. Place on a baking sheet in one layer, cover, and refrigerate until ready to cook.

FOR THE CILANTRO CREAM

Combine the sour cream, cilantro, salt, and pepper in a food processor until smooth. Transfer to a serving bowl, cover with plastic wrap, and refrigerate until ready to use.

Use the olive oil to grease a nonstick griddle over medium heat. Gently blot the grits cakes with paper towels to make sure they are not damp. Cook the cakes 4 to 5 minutes on each side, until golden brown. Garnish with cilantro cream.

YIELD: 15 CAKES (6-8 SERVINGS)
PREP TIME: 5 MINUTES
INACTIVE PREP TIME: 2 HOURS TO OVERNIGHT
COOK TIME: 40 MINUTES

SALADS

Use these recipes as a guide, but improvise with ingredients that are in season and available in your local market. I love to go to the farm stand and buy all sorts of fresh vegetables to make a chopped salad.

Salads

BISTRO SALAD

CUCUMBER SALAD

EGG SALAD

GREEN PESTO PASTA SALAD

CHICKEN CLUB SALAD

LOBSTER SALAD

CHOPPED SALAD

WATERMELON "GREEK" SALAD

BEET AND ARUGULA SALAD

BUTTERMILK COLESLAW

HOPPIN' JOHN SALAD

BROCCOLI SALAD

LAYERED PEA SALAD

COUNTRY SALAD

SUGAR SNAP PEA AND RADISH SALAD

BISTRO SALAD

When I dine in Paris, I always order a *salade verte* (green salad) to start, even if it's not on the menu. I know it sounds kind of boring to be in the culinary mecca of the world and eating salads at every meal, but they're so good. The French really know how to do a salad. The secret is to keep it simple.

1 head of Bibb lettuce, torn into bite-size pieces

Handful of chopped mixed fresh herbs such as chives, tarragon, and parsley, (about ¼ cup)

3 tablespoons extra virgin olive oil

2 tablespoons champagne vinegar

1 teaspoon Dijon mustard

2 tablespoons minced shallots

¾ teaspoon kosher salt

¼ teaspoon freshly ground black pepper

Combine the lettuce and herbs in a medium bowl. In a glass jar or plastic container with a tight-fitting lid, combine the olive oil, vinegar, Dijon mustard, shallots, salt, and pepper. Shake to combine. Pour over the salad and toss. Serve immediately.

YIELD: 4 SERVINGS
PREP TIME: 15 MINUTES

CUCUMBER SALAD

I snack on cucumbers all summer long. I love their fresh flavor, and I believe their high water content helps keep me hydrated. This salad is so nice on a hot afternoon. I like to serve it alongside poached salmon.

2 English cucumbers, peeled and sliced about ⅛-inch thick

⅓ cup sour cream

1 tablespoon minced shallots

2 teaspoons fresh lemon juice

½ teaspoon kosher salt

¼ teaspoon freshly ground black pepper

Place the cucumbers in a large bowl. In a small bowl, combine the sour cream, shallots, lemon juice, salt, and pepper. Mix well. Add the sour cream mixture to the cucumbers and toss to coat.

Serve on its own
or on a bed of lettuce.

YIELD: 4 TO 6 SERVINGS
PREP TIME: 5 MINUTES

EGG SALAD

Egg salad is one of the easiest, most satisfying recipes that I make. I like to eat it piled high on a piece of toasted rye bread with a slice of ripe tomato.

In a large bowl, chop the eggs. Mix in the mayo, mustard, scallions, salt, and pepper.

Serve on toasted bread, or atop a bed of greens or with tomato wedges.

YIELD: 4 SERVINGS
PREP TIME: 5 MINUTES

12 large hard-boiled eggs, shells removed

½ cup mayonnaise

1 tablespoon yellow prepared mustard

4 scallions, green parts only, thinly sliced

½ teaspoon kosher salt

½ teaspoon freshly ground black pepper

GREEN PESTO PASTA SALAD

This recipe was inspired by my mother, who asks me almost daily, "Have you had your greens yet today?" I grow basil in my garden and I always have a surplus, so I make this pesto often. By combining the basil with spinach, I am sneaking in another leafy green vegetable. The pesto freezes nicely, so if your garden is overrun with basil like mine is, make extra and freeze it in ice cube trays. You can pop out cubes for individual servings later. This pasta salad is great on any summer buffet.

1 pound bow tie pasta, or fusilli, penne, or any short pasta

1 loosely packed cup baby spinach

2 packed cups fresh basil leaves

2 garlic cloves

⅛ teaspoon freshly grated nutmeg

¼ cup pine nuts

½ cup extra virgin olive oil

½ cup grated Parmesan cheese, plus more for garnish

½ teaspoon kosher salt

¼ teaspoon freshly ground black pepper

2 cups assorted green vegetables (peas, asparagus tips, broccoli, green beans), blanched

Bring a large pot of salted water to a boil. Add the pasta and cook according to package instructions. Drain and set aside in a large bowl.

Meanwhile, in a food processor, combine the spinach, basil, garlic, nutmeg, and pine nuts. Process until finely chopped. With the motor running, slowly pour in the olive oil until combined. Transfer the mixture to a small bowl and stir in the Parmesan, salt, and pepper.

Blanch the vegetables in boiling water to soften their textures. Add the blanched vegetables and pesto to the pasta. Stir until well combined. Garnish with freshly grated Parmesan. Serve immediately.

YIELD: 6 TO 8 SERVINGS
PREP TIME: 10 MINUTES
COOK TIME: 10 MINUTES

CHICKEN CLUB SALAD

Whenever I'm ordering room service at hotels, I order a club sandwich. They're pretty consistent and usually a safe choice. The best room-service club sandwich is at the Ritz Carlton on Central Park South in New York City. They use all of the traditional elements of a club sandwich but add avocado. I think it might be the only room-service food I've ever craved. I decided to try making their sandwich into a salad at home.

Preheat oven to 400° F.

Place the chicken in a baking dish, drizzle with olive oil, and season with salt and pepper. Roast until cooked all the way through, about 30 minutes. Cool to the touch. Remove and discard the skin and bones, and cut the chicken into chunks.

Meanwhile, cook the bacon in a medium skillet over medium-high heat until crispy. Drain on paper towels. Cool to the touch, then crumble.

In a large bowl, combine the avocado and lemon juice. Add the chicken, bacon, mayo, scallions, mustard, parsley, 1 teaspoon salt, and ¼ teaspoon pepper. Stir until combined. Serve on a bed of lettuce, garnished with tomato wedges.

YIELD: 4 TO 6 SERVINGS
PREP TIME: 10 MINUTES
COOK TIME: 30 MINUTES

4 bone-in, skin-on chicken breast halves

1 tablespoon olive oil

1 teaspoon kosher salt

¼ teaspoon freshly ground black pepper

4 slices applewood-smoked bacon, cut into ½-inch pieces

1 ripe Haas avocado, peeled and diced

3 tablespoons fresh lemon juice

½ cup mayonnaise

¼ cup chopped scallions

2 teaspoons Dijon mustard

2 tablespoons chopped fresh flat-leaf parsley

Bibb lettuce leaves

2 tomatoes, cut into wedges

LOBSTER SALAD

When I moved to the Hamptons, I had to adapt to many lifestyle changes. The biggest for me though was probably sticker shock. Prices for everything are so inflated. I thought I needed glasses when I saw lobster salad at the local market for a whopping $100 a pound. I don't care how much money you have, there is no need to pay that kind of price for lobster salad when it's so easy to make! You can buy cooked lobster meat at the fish market or steam the lobster yourself for a fraction of the price. This recipe also works great with shrimp.

Toss all ingredients in a medium bowl until combined.

Serve on a bed of greens, on a hot dog bun, or with tomato aspic (page 31).

YIELD: 4 SERVINGS
PREP TIME: 5 MINUTES

1 pound cooked lobster meat, cut into chunks (about 4 cups)

Juice of 1 lemon (about 2 tablespoons)

½ cup mayonnaise

1 celery stalk, finely diced

2 tablespoons minced fresh chives

½ teaspoon kosher salt

¼ teaspoon freshly ground black pepper

CHOPPED SALAD

This salad is like one big antipasto. I love the combination of the garlicky, salty salami and spicy pepperoncini, cooled by the provolone cheese and paired with the crisp iceberg lettuce. I make the vinaigrette heavy on the vinegar—equal parts vinegar and oil—because the acidity helps balance the strong flavors of the salad.

For the salad

1 head of iceberg lettuce, chopped

1 English cucumber, chopped

1 red bell pepper, chopped

1 cup canned chickpeas, drained, rinsed

1 cup chopped salami

1 cup chopped provolone cheese

One 6-ounce jar marinated artichoke hearts, drained and chopped

½ medium red onion, finely minced

1 cup cherry tomatoes, halved

8 whole pepperoncini

For the vinaigrette

¼ cup extra virgin olive oil

¼ cup red wine vinegar

1 teaspoon minced fresh rosemary

1 garlic clove, minced

1 teaspoon kosher salt

½ teaspoon freshly ground black pepper

Mix all the salad ingredients in a large bowl.

Combine the vinaigrette ingredients in a small bowl or small glass jar or plastic container with a tight-fitting lid. Whisk together or shake well.

Toss the salad with the vinaigrette and serve immediately.

YIELD: 8 TO 10 SERVINGS
PREP TIME: 20 MINUTES

WATERMELON "GREEK" SALAD

I love the combination of salty and sweet flavors. It is very common in the South to sprinkle salt on your watermelon, so the idea of a salty watermelon salad is not that out of the ordinary for me. Substituting watermelon for the tomatoes in a traditional Greek salad is a great way to add a twist to a classic and surprise the taste buds of your dining partners.

For the salad

6 cups romaine lettuce, torn into pieces (from about 2 hearts of romaine)

3 cups cubed seedless watermelon

1 cup cubed feta cheese (about 4 ounces)

½ cup pitted Kalamata olives (about 2 ½ ounces)

½ medium red onion, very thinly sliced

For the dressing

⅓ cup extra virgin olive oil

3 tablespoons red wine vinegar

Pinch of dried oregano

1 teaspoon kosher salt

¼ teaspoon freshly ground black pepper

In a large salad bowl, combine the romaine, watermelon, feta, olives, and red onion.

In a separate bowl, whisk the dressing ingredients until well blended.

Toss the salad with the dressing and serve immediately.

YIELD: 4 TO 6 SERVINGS
PREP TIME: 10 MINUTES

BEET AND ARUGULA SALAD

I usually make this salad in the early fall when beets are still in season and the air starts to cool. I love the taste of the sweet beets with the peppery arugula and salty blue cheese. If you prefer a milder flavor, try substituting goat cheese.

2 large red beets, washed and stems trimmed to 1 inch

2 large golden beets, washed and stems trimmed to 1 inch

⅓ cup zinfandel vinegar, or any red wine vinegar

1 tablespoon Dijon mustard

1 shallot, minced (about 3 tablespoons)

2 tablespoons fresh lemon juice

1 teaspoon chopped fresh thyme leaves

2 teaspoons kosher salt

1 teaspoon freshly ground black pepper

⅔ cup extra virgin olive oil

½ red onion, thinly sliced

6 cups baby arugula (about 8 ounces)

¼ cup crumbled blue cheese

¼ cup chopped toasted walnuts

Bring a medium pot of water to a boil over high heat. Add the beets and boil until fork tender, 45 to 60 minutes depending on the size of the beets. Drain and set aside until cool enough to handle.

While the beets are cooling, make the vinaigrette. In a blender, combine the vinegar, mustard, shallot, lemon juice, thyme, salt, and pepper. With the machine running, slowly drizzle in the olive oil until emulsified. Set aside.

After beets have cooled, gently remove their skin using your fingertips. Thinly slice each beet. Place the beets and onions in a medium bowl and gently toss with the vinaigrette. Cover and set aside at room temperature for at least 1 hour and up to 4 hours.

To serve, evenly divide the arugula onto serving plates. Top with the beet and onion mixture. Sprinkle each salad with blue cheese and toasted walnuts. Drizzle the arugula with any leftover vinaigrette, if desired.

YIELD: 4 TO 6 SERVINGS
PREP TIME: 30 MINUTES
INACTIVE PREP TIME: 1 TO 4 HOURS
COOK TIME: 60 MINUTES

SUGAR SNAP PEA AND RADISH SALAD

The bright colors of this salad make it the perfect addition to any summer spread. I love the combination of the sweet snap peas with the peppery radishes.

Bring a medium pot of salted water to a boil. Blanch the peas just until tender-crisp and bright green, 2 to 3 minutes. Remove the peas from the pot and cool in ice water. Drain well. In a large salad bowl, combine the peas, radishes, and chives.

In a small glass jar or plastic container with a tight-fitting lid, combine the olive oil, vinegar, honey, salt, and pepper. Shake to combine.

Toss the vinaigrette with the salad and serve.

YIELD: 4 SERVINGS
PREP TIME: 15 MINUTES
COOK TIME: 3 MINUTES

For the salad

¾ pound sugar snap peas, trimmed

1 bunch radishes, trimmed and leaves removed (I like to cut half of the radishes into quarters, and thinly slice the other half to create different textures)

2 tablespoons minced fresh chives

For the vinaigrette

3 tablespoons olive oil

1 tablespoon cider vinegar

1 teaspoon honey

1 teaspoon kosher salt

½ teaspoon freshly ground black pepper

SOUPS

What is more comforting than a warm bowl of soup on a winter's day, or more refreshing than a chilled soup in the heat of the summer? Soups are a terrific way to use seasonal vegetables. Be inventive and try blending roasted root vegetables or pureeing raw summer vegetables.

Soups can be very elegant, especially at a cocktail party when served in shot glasses or espresso cups, or as a first course at dinner in a beautiful bowl. I like to add a garnish of fresh herbs, sour cream, or homemade croutons to complement the flavor and presentation of the soup.

Soups

SAUSAGE AND LENTIL STEW

ROASTED CARROT AND GINGER SOUP

CHILI

GAZPACHO

PINTO BEAN SOUP

SCALLOP-CORN CHOWDER

MOM'S VEGETABLE SOUP

ROASTED TOMATO SOUP

BUTTERNUT SQUASH SOUP

CHILLED CUCUMBER SOUP

ASIAN CHICKEN-NOODLE SOUP

SAUSAGE AND LENTIL STEW

This just might be my favorite recipe. I am a huge fan of lentils and I love combining them with sausage. I find that using andouille sausage gives the stew an added layer of spicy flavor, but other sausages can be substituted. It is even better the next day.

In a large heavy pot, cook the bacon over medium heat until fat is rendered and the bacon is crisp, about 7 minutes. Remove the bacon pieces and drain on paper towels. Reserve for garnishing.

Add the onion, carrots, celery, and bay leaves to the bacon fat. Turn the heat to medium-low and cook the vegetables, stirring frequently, until very tender, about 15 minutes.

Stir in the lentils, sausage, and kale. Add the tomatoes, crushing the tomatoes with your fingers as you add them to the pot. Add the chicken stock, salt, and pepper. Bring the mixture to a boil over high heat. Reduce the heat to low and simmer for 1 hour, covered, until lentils are tender. Stir and add more salt and pepper to taste, as desired.

Ladle into bowls and top with the reserved bacon bits and some grated cheese. Serve immediately.

YIELD: ABOUT 12 CUPS (6 TO 8 SERVINGS)
PREP TIME: 20 MINUTES
COOK TIME: 1 HOUR 20 MINUTES.

3 slices thick-cut bacon, diced (about 4 ounces)

1 large yellow onion, diced (about 1½ cups)

3 large carrots, diced (about 1¼ cups)

3 celery stalks, diced (about 1 cup)

2 bay leaves

8 ounces French lentils

1 pound andouille sausage, cut into ¼-inch-thick diagonal slices

2 cups coarsely chopped fresh kale

One 28-ounce can whole tomatoes, with juice

6 cups low-sodium chicken broth

2 teaspoons kosher salt

½ teaspoon freshly ground black pepper

Grated Asiago or Parmesan cheese

ROASTED CARROT AND GINGER SOUP

Roasting carrots brings out all of their sweetness. For this soup, I added some ginger for a spicy contrast, and the bay leaves and Worcestershire sauce make a rich backdrop of flavor. With plain yogurt instead of heavy cream, it still has a creamy texture without all of the fat.

About 1½ pounds carrots, cut in large dice (4 cups)

2 tablespoons olive oil

Kosher salt and freshly ground black pepper

1 tablespoon unsalted butter

1 medium yellow onion, diced

1 tablespoon finely minced fresh ginger

2 bay leaves

1 quart low-sodium chicken broth

1 tablespoon fresh lemon juice

1 tablespoon Worcestershire sauce

½ cup plain yogurt

Minced fresh flat-leaf parsley

Preheat oven to 400° F. Line a baking sheet with parchment paper.

Toss the carrots with the 1 tablespoon olive oil, season with salt and pepper, and spread on the baking sheet. Roast until fork tender, about 20 minutes.

Meanwhile, in a stockpot or Dutch oven, heat the remaining 1 tablespoon olive oil and the butter over medium-high heat. Sauté the onions, ginger, and bay leaves until the onions are translucent, about 5 minutes. Add the chicken broth, lemon juice, Worcestershire, ½ teaspoon salt, and ½ teaspoon pepper, and bring to a low boil. Add the carrots, reduce to a simmer, and cook about 10 minutes. Remove the bay leaves. Use an immersion blender or transfer to a blender in batches and blend until creamy. Add the yogurt and blend to combine. Serve garnished with fresh parsley.

YIELD: 4 TO 6 SERVINGS
PREP TIME: 20 MINUTES
COOK TIME: 40 MINUTES

SCALLOP-CORN CHOWDER

People in New England love their clam chowder. I took inspiration from the traditional to create my own version, using scallops and fresh corn. I don't use heavy cream, so this chowder has a lighter taste, making it perfect for summer dining when corn is in season.

In a large Dutch oven over medium heat, melt the butter. Add the onions and carrots. Cook until onions are translucent and carrots are tender, about 8 minutes. Stir in the flour and cook 2 minutes. Add the salt, pepper, thyme, bay leaf, chicken broth, and 2 cups of the corn. Stir to combine and bring to a simmer.

Meanwhile, in a blender combine the remaining 2 cups corn and the milk. Add to the soup. Let simmer about 5 minutes. Add scallops and cook 3 minutes. Remove the bay leaf and thyme stem. Garnish with bacon and scallions, if desired, and serve immediately.

YIELD: 4 SERVINGS
PREP TIME: 10 MINUTES
COOK TIME: 20 MINUTES

4 tablespoons (½ stick) unsalted butter

1 medium yellow onion, finely diced

1 large carrot, finely diced

1 tablespoon all-purpose flour

½ teaspoon kosher salt

¼ teaspoon freshly ground black pepper

1 sprig of fresh thyme

1 bay leaf

One 14-ounce can low-sodium chicken broth

4 cups fresh corn kernels (about 6 ears)

2 cups milk

1 pound sea scallops, halved, or quartered if large

Crumbled cooked bacon and sliced scallions, optional

BUTTERNUT SQUASH SOUP

When I make this soup, my kitchen fills with the scents of autumn. Butternut squash and apples are both in season in the fall, and when they're cooked with garlic and thyme, the aroma is intoxicating. After you blend all of the ingredients, it becomes a beautiful golden orange hue. I like serving this soup as a first course at fall dinner parties, or in espresso cups with a dollop of sour cream for larger groups.

One 2 to 2½-pound butternut squash, peeled and cut into 1½-inch cubes (about 4 cups)

1 large apple (such as Gala or Jonagold), peeled, cored and cut into sixths

1 medium yellow onion, cut into sixths

2 tablespoons olive oil

1 teaspoon kosher salt

½ teaspoon freshly ground black pepper

1 garlic clove

4 sprigs fresh thyme

1 bay leaf

4 cups low-sodium chicken broth

Preheat oven to 400° F. Line a baking sheet with parchment paper or foil.

Place the squash, apple, and onion on the baking sheet. Drizzle with the olive oil, season with the salt and pepper, and toss to combine. Roast in the oven until fork tender, 40 to 45 minutes.

Make a sachet with the garlic, thyme, and bay leaf (tied in a bundle using cheesecloth and cotton twine). Bring chicken broth and sachet to a low boil in a stockpot over high heat. Add the squash, apple, and onion. Lower the heat to a simmer and cook about 20 minutes. Remove from heat and remove the sachet. Use an immersion blender, or transfer to a blender in batches, and blend until smooth and creamy. Season the soup with additional salt and pepper to taste. Serve immediately.

YIELD: 4 SERVINGS
PREP TIME: 15 MINUTES
COOK TIME: 65 MINUTES

CHILLED CUCUMBER SOUP

On a hot summer's day, this soup is an excellent choice for lunch. I also like serving it in a shot glass as a passed hors d'oeuvre at cocktail parties. The sweetness of the cucumbers is wonderful with the tartness of the yogurt and sour cream.

Place half the cucumbers, yogurt, sour cream, chicken broth, mint, chopped chives, mustard, lemon juice, and salt in a blender. Pulse until blended. Add the remaining cucumbers and blend until smooth. Transfer to a pitcher or bowl and chill until serving time. Garnish with crabmeat or shrimp and minced chives, if desired.

YIELD: 4 TO 6 SERVINGS
PREP TIME: 10 MINUTES

3 English cucumbers, peeled and roughly chopped

1 cup Greek-style plain yogurt

⅓ cup sour cream

½ cup low-sodium chicken broth

2 tablespoons chopped fresh mint

2 tablespoons chopped fresh chives

½ teaspoon dry mustard

1 tablespoon fresh lemon juice

½ teaspoon kosher salt

Lump crabmeat or poached shrimp, and minced chives, optional

ASIAN CHICKEN-NOODLE SOUP

While on a girls' trip on my friend Wendi's boat, I had an Asian-style chicken-noodle soup. I came home and tried to copy it, but I couldn't quite get the flavors right. After a few attempts, I finally mastered it and came up with this recipe. I like it spicy, so I serve extra chili sauce on the side.

1 tablespoon vegetable oil

½ medium yellow onion, minced

1 garlic clove, thinly sliced

1 tablespoon grated fresh peeled ginger

6 cups low-sodium chicken broth

3 stalks lemongrass, the bottom 3 inches only, each stalk cut into three 1-inch pieces

1 teaspoon sriracha or chili-garlic chili sauce

Juice of 1 lime (about 2 tablespoons)

2 tablespoons soy sauce

2 teaspoons toasted sesame oil

2 chicken breast halves, pounded to ¼-inch thick and thinly sliced

2 cups thinly sliced napa cabbage (about ½ head)

1 cup shredded carrots (1 to 2 medium)

1 cup thinly sliced red bell pepper (1 medium)

One 3 to 4-ounce package rice noodles, prepared to package instructions

Cilantro and mint leaves, sliced scallions, and bean sprouts

In a stockpot over medium heat, heat the oil. Add the onions, garlic, and ginger. Sauté until the onions are translucent, 7 to 8 minutes. Add the chicken broth, lemongrass, chili sauce, lime juice, soy sauce, and sesame oil. Simmer for 10 minutes. Increase the heat to a low boil, add the chicken, and cook about 5 minutes. Add the cabbage, carrots, and red pepper, and simmer an additional 2 to 3 minutes.

Divide the rice noodles among bowls and ladle the soup into each bowl. Garnish with cilantro, mint, scallions, and bean sprouts, and serve with additional chili sauce, if desired.

YIELD: 4 TO 6 SERVINGS
PREP TIME: 10 MINUTES
COOK TIME: 25 MINUTES

ENTREES

My taste in food is like my taste in fashion—comfortable and classic with a touch of couture. Many of the following entrees are classic comfort food recipes from my family that I have updated and refined. The entree is the heart of the meal. And I find that people tend to like simple foods made with the finest quality ingredients the best.

SLOW-COOKER PULLED-PORK BARBECUE

APRICOT-GLAZED BRAISED PORK CHOPS

CHICKEN AND DUMPLINGS

LOGAN COUNTY HAMBURGERS

MEDITERRANEAN PASTA

CRISPY OVEN-ROASTED CHICKEN WITH ROASTED
GARLIC, PANCETTA, AND ROSEMARY

CHICKEN POT PIE

TURKEY SHEPHERD'S PIE

CORNFLAKE-CRUSTED HALIBUT
WITH TOMATO-AVOCADO-CORN RELISH

MEAT LOAF

SPAGHETTI WITH MEAT SAUCE

APRICOT-GLAZED BRAISED PORK CHOPS

This super-simple recipe is great for a weeknight meal in a hurry. The apricot glaze, made from jam, takes just moments to make but tastes complex due to the spicy Dijon mustard and tangy vinegar. Quickly braising the chops keeps the meat tender and moist.

1 cup low-sodium chicken stock

2 teaspoons Dijon mustard

1 tablespoon red wine vinegar

¼ cup apricot jam

2 tablespoons olive oil

6 boneless center-cut pork chops (about 1¼ inches thick), trimmed of fat

Kosher salt and freshly ground black pepper

1 garlic clove, smashed

1 bay leaf

In a medium bowl, whisk together the chicken stock, mustard, vinegar, and jam.

Heat the olive oil in a large skillet over medium-high heat. Season the pork chops with salt and pepper. Place the pork chops in the hot oil and brown about 3 minutes per side.

Remove the pork chops from pan and set aside. Add the chicken stock mixture to the pan and deglaze the pan, scraping up the brown bits with a wooden spoon. Add the garlic clove and bay leaf. Reduce heat to a simmer. Return the pork chops to the pan, cover and braise until just cooked through, about 5 minutes.

Transfer the pork chops to a serving dish and tent lightly with foil to keep warm. Discard the garlic and bay leaf. Bring the liquid to a rapid boil and reduce to a thick glaze, about 3 minutes. Season to taste with salt and freshly ground black pepper. Pour the glaze over the pork chops and serve.

YIELD: 6 SERVINGS
PREP TIME: 5 MINUTES
COOK TIME: 15 MINUTES

CRISPY OVEN-ROASTED CHICKEN WITH ROASTED GARLIC, PANCETTA, AND ROSEMARY

In East Hampton, New York, there is a very popular restaurant called Nick and Toni's. The food is great, but a lot of people go for the scene. Me? I go for the chicken. They cook the chicken in an iron skillet inside of a wood-burning oven. Simply seasoned with salt and pepper and roasted with pancetta, garlic cloves, and fresh rosemary, its skin is perfectly crisp and the succulent meat rich with flavor. I created this recipe during the off-season when I was dreaming of feasting at Nick and Toni's.

Preheat the oven to 400° F. Rinse the chicken and pat dry completely. Heavily salt and pepper each piece. Set aside.

In a medium ovenproof skillet over medium heat, cook the pancetta until crispy, about 6 minutes. Remove with a slotted spoon and set aside. Drain off all but 1 tablespoon of the fat. Add the olive oil and garlic cloves. Cook until the cloves are golden brown. Transfer to oven and bake until the cloves are soft, 5 to 7 minutes. Carefully remove the pan from the oven and set aside.

Meanwhile, in a large ovenproof skillet, heat 1 inch of canola oil over high heat until very hot but not smoking. Carefully place the chicken skin side down in the hot oil. Let cook 3 to 4 minutes to start crisping the skin. Do not turn. Carefully transfer the pan to the oven and bake until the chicken is cooked all the way through, 7 to 8 minutes. Carefully remove the pan from the oven.

Transfer the chicken to a serving platter. Sprinkle the top with pancetta, garlic cloves, and fresh rosemary.

YIELD: 6 SERVINGS
PREP TIME: 5 MINUTES
COOK TIME: 25 MINUTES

6 boneless, skin-on chicken breast halves

Kosher salt and freshly ground black pepper

½ pound pancetta or slab bacon, cut in ½-inch cubes

1 tablespoon olive oil

15 garlic cloves

Canola oil

1 tablespoon chopped fresh rosemary, plus sprigs

CHICKEN POT PIE

I always used to make my chicken pot pies with a traditional pastry crust or with biscuits, but I decided to try using puff pastry when I was on my flat pie kick (see page 17). One bite of that flaky, buttery crust with the creamy filling and my mind was made up—I would be using puff pastry on my chicken pot pies for good. I love making individual pot pies in ovenproof bowls so that everyone can have their own. They are perfect for a winter dinner party.

One 14 to 17-ounce good-quality puff pastry (such as Dufour), thawed according to package instructions

1 quart low-sodium chicken broth

1 large yellow onion, quartered

2 bay leaves

1 teaspoon whole black peppercorns

3 sprigs fresh thyme, plus 1 tablespoon chopped

4 boneless, skinless chicken breast halves

3 tablespoons unsalted butter

½ cup peeled fresh pearl onions

2 medium diced carrots

1 cup sliced white mushrooms

1 cup fresh or thawed frozen peas

5 tablespoons all-purpose flour

1 cup milk

1 teaspoon kosher salt

½ teaspoon freshly ground black pepper

1 large egg, lightly beaten

YIELD: 4 SERVINGS
PREP TIME: 1 HOUR
COOK TIME: 35 MINUTES

Line a baking sheet with parchment paper. On a lightly floured surface, roll out the pastry dough with a floured rolling pin. Transfer to the baking sheet, cover with plastic wrap and refrigerate while preparing pie filling.

Combine the broth, quartered onion, bay leaves, peppercorns, and thyme sprigs in a large pot over high heat. Bring to a boil, reduce the heat, and simmer for 30 minutes. Add the chicken breasts. Raise the heat and return to a boil. Reduce heat and simmer until the chicken is just cooked through, about 10 to 15 minutes.

Transfer chicken to a plate and set aside. Strain the stock and set aside 2½ cups. Reserve the remaining stock for another use. When the chicken is cool to the touch, cut it into bite-size chunks and set aside.

Preheat the oven to 375° F.

Melt the butter in a large skillet over medium heat. Add the pearl onions and carrots. Cook, stirring occasionally, for about 5 minutes. Add the mushrooms and peas and cook another 5 minutes. Stir in the flour and cook 1 minute more. Add the reserved stock and the milk, stirring constantly. Cook until the sauce begins to thicken, about 5 minutes. Remove from the heat and add the chicken, the chopped thyme, salt, and pepper. Set aside.

Remove the pastry from the refrigerator and set out four 2-cup individual ovenproof bowls. Using one of the empty bowls as a guide, cut the pastry into four circles. Spoon the filling into each bowl and place one circle on each pot pie, pressing around the edges to seal the pastry to the bowl. Cut a vent in the center. Using a pastry brush, brush the entire surface of each pie with egg.

Bake until the pastry is puffed and dark golden brown, about 35 minutes.

TURKEY SHEPHERD'S PIE

The day after Thanksgiving, I'm always trying to come up with creative ways to use my leftovers. With this spin on shepherd's pie, I use not only my turkey, but also my leftover mashed potatoes, veggies, and broth. If it's not that time of year, this recipe also works great with chicken. For a quick and easy dinner, pick up a large rotisserie chicken from the grocery store and substitute it for the turkey meat.

6 tablespoons (¾ stick) unsalted butter

1½ cups diced carrots (about 3 carrots)

1 cup diced celery (about 2 stalks)

1 large yellow onion, minced

1 cup thinly sliced white button mushrooms (about 4 ounces)

One 10-ounce package frozen peas, thawed (about 2 cups)

4 cups shredded cooked turkey

1½ teaspoons finely minced fresh thyme

1 teaspoon finely minced fresh sage

2 teaspoons kosher salt

1 teaspoon freshly ground black pepper

3 tablespoons all-purpose flour

2½ cups low-sodium turkey or chicken broth

6 cups mashed potatoes (leftover or use recipe on page 124)

3 tablespoons grated Parmesan cheese

Preheat the oven to 350° F. Grease a 13 by 9 by 2-inch baking dish.

Melt 3 tablespoons of the butter in a large heavy skillet over medium-high heat. Add the carrots, celery, onions, and mushrooms. Cook until vegetables begin to soften, about 10 minutes. Add the peas, turkey, thyme, sage, salt, and pepper. Mix well, remove from the heat, and set aside.

Melt the remaining 3 tablespoons butter in a medium saucepan over medium heat. Add flour and cook, stirring, for 2 minutes. Add stock slowly and bring to a low boil. Reduce the heat and cook until the sauce thickens, about 3 minutes. Add the sauce to the vegetable-turkey mixture and mix well. Transfer to the baking dish.

Spoon the mashed potatoes on top, spreading gently to cover. Sprinkle with the Parmesan. Bake until the potatoes are lightly browned, about 1 hour.

YIELD: 6 TO 8 SERVINGS
PREP TIME: 30 MINUTES
COOK TIME: 1 HOUR

CORNFLAKE-CRUSTED HALIBUT WITH TOMATO-AVOCADO-CORN RELISH

I love anything deep fried, especially fish, but eating too much of it can take a toll on a girl's waist line. I created this fried fish alternative once when I was on a diet and having a bad craving for the real thing. The crust was crisp, the fish moist and flaky—I didn't even miss all the fat! In the summertime, I love pairing the fish with this tomato-avocado-corn relish. The relish is so good, that I sometimes increase the recipe and serve it as a side dish. Don't be afraid to experiment with the cornflakes either. I love making this dish with chicken as well.

Preheat oven to 325° F. Grease a baking sheet.

In a resealable plastic bag, crush the cornflakes. Add the paprika, ½ teaspoon salt, ¼ teaspoon pepper, and the cayenne. Transfer to a shallow dish. In another shallow dish, whisk the eggs and egg white to combine.

Season the halibut fillets with salt and pepper. Dip each fillet in the eggs and dredge in the cornflake mixture. Place the fish on the baking sheet and bake until the fish is opaque and flakes with a fork, about 15 minutes.

While the fish is baking, mix all of the relish ingredients in a small bowl. Set aside.

Place the halibut on a serving plate and spoon the relish on top. Serve immediately.

YIELD: 4 SERVINGS
PREP TIME: 20 MINUTES
COOK TIME: 15 MINUTES

For the fish

4 cups cornflakes

½ teaspoon paprika

Kosher salt and freshly ground black pepper

¼ teaspoon cayenne pepper

3 whole eggs

1 egg white

4 halibut fillets, ½-pound each

For the relish

2 ears fresh corn, shucked, kernels cut from the cob (about 1½ cups)

1 cup cherry tomatoes, halved

1 avocado, seeded, peeled, and chopped

8 fresh basil leaves, chiffonade (about ⅓ cup)

3 tablespoons olive oil

½ tablespoon red wine vinegar

¾ teaspoon kosher salt

¼ teaspoon freshly ground black pepper

MEAT LOAF

I like to call meat loaf "man loaf" because it's every man's favorite dish. My husband loves when I make meat loaf, and it makes the best leftovers. We love it the next day on white bread with mayonnaise.

1 tablespoon olive oil

½ medium, yellow onion, diced (about ¾ cup)

1 garlic clove, minced

1 medium red pepper, finely diced (about 1 cup)

1 bay leaf

2 tablespoons chopped fresh flat-leaf parsley

2 teaspoons chopped fresh thyme

2 pounds lean ground beef

2 large eggs, lightly beaten

¾ cup dry bread crumbs

1 cup ketchup

1 tablespoon Worcestershire sauce

2 teaspoons kosher salt

1 teaspoon freshly ground black pepper

Preheat the oven 350° F. Line a baking sheet with parchment paper. Spray lightly with oil.

Heat the olive oil in a medium skillet over medium heat. Sauté the onions, garlic, and bay leaf until the onions are tender, about 3 minutes. Add the red pepper and cook until the red pepper is tender, about 5 minutes more. Stir in the parsley and thyme and cook for another 2 minutes. Remove pan from the heat and let the onion mixture cool. Discard the bay leaf.

In a large bowl, combine the beef, eggs, bread crumbs, ½ cup of the ketchup, the Worcestershire sauce, salt, pepper, and the cooled vegetables. Use your hands to mix everything together.

Transfer the mixture to the center of the baking sheet and form into a "loaf." Coat the meat loaf with the remaining ½ cup ketchup.

Bake for 1 to 1½ hours (depending on the shape of your loaf), until the meat loaf is firm. Let set for about 5 minutes before slicing.

YIELD: 6 SERVINGS
PREP TIME: 20 MINUTES
COOK TIME: 1 TO 1½ HOURS

SPAGHETTI WITH MEAT SAUCE

There is a restaurant in Huntington, West Virginia, called Jim's Spaghetti House. I grew up eating there, and every time I go home, I have to make at least one stop for a meal there. Their spaghetti sauce is a secret, and everyone in town is always trading recipes, each claiming to know what goes into the sauce. I've yet to taste any that are just like Jim's, but this one comes pretty darn close.

In a stockpot or Dutch oven, combine the beef (do not brown first), onion, tomato paste, tomato sauce, 2 cups water, the sugar, chili powder, garlic salt, salt, and pepper. Mix until combined. Add the bay leaves. Cover and simmer over medium-low heat for approximately 2 hours. Stir in the vinegar and simmer another 30 minutes.

Meanwhile, bring a large pot of salted water to a boil. Add spaghetti and cook until al dente. Drain.

Toss the spaghetti with the sauce. Serve topped with grated Parmesan.

YIELD: 4 TO 6 SERVINGS
PREP TIME: 10 MINUTES
COOK TIME: 2 HOURS 30 MINUTES

2 pounds lean ground beef

1 medium yellow onion, grated

One 12-ounce can tomato paste

One 16-ounce can tomato sauce

2 tablespoons sugar

2 tablespoons chili powder

1 teaspoon garlic salt

1½ teaspoons kosher salt

1 teaspoon freshly ground black pepper

2 bay leaves

1 tablespoon white wine vinegar

1 pound spaghetti

Grated Parmesan cheese

BILLY'S SKIRT STEAKS

One of my husband's specialties is his secret marinade for skirt steaks. The acidity of the lime juice breaks down the meat, making it really tender, while the anchovy paste adds a salty flavor. The olive oil provides a nice flame when the meat hits the grill. I guess it's no longer a secret!

½ cup fresh lime juice (about 6 limes)

½ cup olive oil

8 garlic cloves, finely minced

1½ ounces anchovy paste (about 2½ tablespoons)

2 teaspoons freshly ground black pepper

2 pounds skirt steak

Fresh cilantro

In a mixing bowl, whisk together the lime juice, olive oil, garlic, anchovy paste, and pepper until emulsified. Place the skirt steaks with marinade in a large resealable plastic bag or shallow container and cover. Marinate in the refrigerator for 4 to 6 hours, or up to overnight.

Place a grill pan over medium-high heat or preheat a gas or charcoal grill. Cook the steaks to desired degree of doneness (I think they are best served medium rare). Cut on the diagonal and serve garnished with fresh cilantro.

YIELD: 4 TO 6 SERVINGS
PREP TIME: 10 MINUTES
INACTIVE PREP TIME: 4 HOURS TO OVERNIGHT
COOK TIME: 5 TO 10 MINUTES

BEEF STEW

I always brag about my grandma's cooking, but my grandpa was also a great cook. He perfected a couple of recipes that we all really enjoyed. When my grandma went to college in her sixties, he found himself cooking a lot more. This one-pot wonder was one of his standbys, and he always served it with coleslaw and cornbread.

Season the beef generously with salt and pepper. Sprinkle the beef with 2 tablespoons of the flour and toss to evenly coat all sides.

Heat the olive oil in a large Dutch oven or large heavy pot over medium-high heat. Add the beef in a single layer (do in two batches, if necessary) and brown on all sides, about 5 minutes (per batch). Remove the beef from the pan, and set aside in a bowl. Pour the cider vinegar into the pot. Using a wooden spoon, scrape up all the brown bits from the bottom of the pot. Return all the beef to the pot. Add the potatoes, onions, carrots, celery, and broths. Bring to a boil, reduce the heat to very low, and simmer, covered, until the beef is very tender, about 2 hours.

In a small bowl, mix ¼ cup of the stew liquid with the remaining 2 tablespoons flour until smooth. Stir into the beef stew. Continue to simmer over low heat and allow the broth to thicken, about 10 minutes. Stir in 1½ teaspoons salt, ¾ teaspoon pepper, and the parsley. Ladle into individual bowls and serve.

YIELD: 4 TO 6 SERVINGS
PREP TIME: 20 MINUTES
COOK TIME: 2 ½ HOURS

2 pounds lean beef, cut into 2-inch cubes

Kosher salt and freshly ground black pepper

¼ cup all-purpose flour

3 tablespoons olive oil

3 tablespoons cider vinegar

4 medium potatoes, cut into 1-inch cubes

2 medium yellow onions, quartered

4 large carrots, cut on the diagonal into 1-inch pieces

1 celery stalk, cut into 1-inch pieces

1 quart low-sodium beef broth

1 cup vegetable broth or water

¼ cup minced fresh flat-leaf parsley

SAUSAGE WITH ONIONS AND GRAPES

I love all of Italy, but if I had to pick a favorite region it would be Tuscany. I had a dish similar to this while visiting the area, and I loved the salty-sweet combination of the sausages and the grapes. It sounds different, but it really works well.

4 sweet or hot Italian sausages

1 tablespoon olive oil

2 large yellow onions, sliced

5 garlic cloves, very thinly sliced

2 cups seedless red grapes

½ cup white wine

3 tablespoons chopped fresh flat-leaf parsley

¾ teaspoon kosher salt

¼ teaspoon freshly ground black pepper

1 tablespoon balsamic vinegar

Bring a medium pot of water to a boil. Simmer the sausages for 8 minutes. Drain on paper towels.

Heat the olive oil in a large skillet over medium heat. Brown the sausages on all sides, about 5 minutes. Transfer the sausages to a plate and cover loosely with foil to keep warm.

Add the onions to the skillet and sauté until tender, about 4 minutes. Add the garlic and cook for another 2 minutes. Add the grapes and cook until their skin begins to pop, about 4 minutes. Add the white wine and simmer until the wine is nearly evaporated. Toss in the parsley, salt, and pepper. Splash the onion-grape mixture with the balsamic vinegar. Serve the sausages whole or sliced on the diagonal on top of the onion mixture.

YIELD: 4 SERVINGS
PREP TIME: 5 MINUTES
COOK TIME: 20 MINUTES

CHICKEN DIVAN

Since my mom worked full-time while I was growing up, we ate most of our meals at my grandparents' home. Mom had a couple of specialties that she would make when she had time, and chicken divan was my favorite. The recipe is pretty healthy, especially if you use low-fat sour cream. It's a great weeknight meal because it's quick to assemble, and it also makes for terrific leftovers. To cut down on cooking time even more, buy a rotisserie chicken at the grocery store.

Preheat oven to 325° F.

In a large pot of boiling salted water cook the broccoli until it is just tender, about 4 to 5 minutes. Cool in ice water. Drain well and set aside.

In a medium saucepan, melt the butter over low heat and stir in the flour. Cook for about 3 minutes. Add the broth and shallots and increase the heat to bring to a boil. Reduce the heat and simmer, stirring occasionally, until the mixture thickens, about 10 minutes. Add the Sherry, salt, pepper, and lemon juice. Remove from the heat and stir in the sour cream and ¼ cup of the Parmesan.

Arrange the broccoli in a 2-quart flameproof baking dish and pour half of the sauce over it. Arrange the chicken on top and pour the remaining sauce over it. Top with bread crumbs and the remaining cheese.

Bake for 20 minutes. Put the dish under the broiler until the bread crumbs are golden brown, about 1 minute.

YIELD: 4 TO 6 SERVINGS
PREP TIME: 15 MINUTES
COOK TIME: 30 MINUTES

1 large bunch broccoli, trimmed and cut into bite-size pieces (about 3 cups)

3 tablespoons unsalted butter

3 tablespoons all-purpose flour

2 cups low-sodium chicken broth

1 shallot, minced

3 tablespoons medium-dry Sherry

1 teaspoon kosher salt

½ teaspoon freshly ground black pepper

1 tablespoon fresh lemon juice

½ cup sour cream

½ cup grated Parmesan cheese

1½ pounds boneless, skinless chicken breast, cooked and shredded

1 cup dry bread crumbs

DIJON-PISTACHIO CRUSTED RACK OF LAMB

Rack of lamb encrusted with Dijon-flavored breadcrumbs is a classic. One night I decided to throw in some ground pistachios, and I loved the bright green color and nutty flavor they added. This is an elegant but easy entree, perfect for a special celebration. You could also cut the recipe in half and serve it as a romantic dinner for two.

2 racks of lamb, (for 3 chops per person) trimmed of fat

Kosher salt and freshly ground black pepper

2 tablespoons olive oil

¼ cup Dijon mustard

1 tablespoon fresh chopped thyme

2 shallots, minced

½ cup dry bread crumbs

¼ cup crushed pistachios

Preheat the oven to 450° F. Season the lamb with salt and pepper. Line a baking sheet with parchment paper.

Place a large heavy ovenproof skillet (I prefer cast-iron) over high heat. Pour in the olive oil. When the oil is hot, place one or two of the lamb racks (depending on the size of your pan), fat side down, into the oil. Sear the meat until golden, about 3 minutes. Turn the meat and brown the other side. Transfer the lamb to a plate or side dish. Repeat if necessary with the other rack.

In a small bowl, combine the Dijon mustard, thyme, and shallots. In a wide, shallow bowl, combine bread crumbs, pistachios, ¼ teaspoon salt, and ¼ teaspoon pepper.

Use a pastry brush to spread the Dijon mixture over the meat side of the lamb rack. Dredge the Dijon-coated lamb rack in the bread crumb mixture. Place the lamb racks on the baking sheet.

Bake for 25 to 30 minutes for rare, or longer depending on the degree of doneness you desire. Loosely cover with foil and let stand ten minutes. Slice and serve.

YIELD: 6 SERVINGS
PREP TIME: 20 MINUTES
INACTIVE PREP TIME: 5 MINUTES
COOK TIME: 25 TO 30 MINUTES

FISHERMAN'S STEW

On Long Island, seafood is a way of life. At our home, I can watch the boats of the commercial fishermen head out and the baymen digging for clams just off the shore. Commercial fishermen have one of the most strenuous and underappreciated jobs. This recipe is dedicated to them.

3 tablespoons olive oil

2 anchovy fillets

1 bay leaf

⅛ teaspoon red pepper flakes

2 garlic cloves, thinly sliced

1 medium yellow onion, chopped

Kosher salt and freshly ground black pepper

One 28-ounce can whole tomatoes, with juice

2 tablespoons chopped fresh flat-leaf parsley

1 pound firm white fish fillets (cod, halibut, or mahi-mahi), cut into large pieces

6 to 8 littleneck clams (be sure to rinse all of the sand off the clams)

6 to 8 large shrimp, peeled and deveined

6 to 8 sea scallops

1½ tablespoons fresh lemon juice

In a large skillet over medium heat, heat olive oil. Add anchovies, bay leaf, and red pepper. Cook until anchovies begin to dissolve, about 2 minutes. Add the garlic, onions, 1 teaspoon salt, and ½ teaspoon pepper. Sauté until onions are translucent, about 10 minutes. Stir in the tomatoes and parsley. Use a wooden spoon to crush the tomatoes into bite-size pieces. Reduce heat and simmer for 10 minutes to blend the flavors. Return the heat to medium.

Season the fish with salt and pepper. Add the fish and clams and gently stir to combine. Cover and cook 4 to 5 minutes. Add the shrimp and scallops and gently stir to combine. Cover and cook an additional 4 to 5 minutes. Stir in the lemon juice and serve immediately.

YIELD: 4 TO 6 SERVINGS
PREP TIME: 10 MINUTES
COOK TIME: 25 MINUTES

TARRAGON-CITRUS MAHI-MAHI

My husband and I spend part of the winter months in Miami. I love all of the fresh seafood that is available, especially the mahi-mahi. I developed this recipe one day using some of that beautiful Florida citrus. The flavor of the citrus and tarragon is very clean and subtle.

Remove the peel, pith, and outer membrane of each piece of fruit. Working over a bowl, slice each into segments and remove the seeds. Dice the segments into the bowl. Stir in the tarragon. Cover and refrigerate until ready to serve.

Season the mahi-mahi with salt and pepper. Heat the oil in a nonstick skillet over high heat. Sear the fish on each side until opaque in the center, about 3 to 4 minutes per side depending on thickness. Transfer the fish to serving plates, top with a large spoonful of the citrus salsa, and serve immediately.

1 pink grapefruit

1 tangerine

1 blood orange, or regular orange

2 tablespoons chopped fresh tarragon

Four (4 to 6 ounce) pieces mahi-mahi

Kosher salt and freshly ground black pepper

2 tablespoons olive oil

Any white fish—grouper, snapper, or halibut—can be substituted.

YIELD: 4 SERVINGS
PREP TIME: 15 MINUTES
COOK TIME: 8 MINUTES

ISLAND SPICE SALMON

Salmon is my favorite fish and I prepare it so many different ways, but this is one of the best, not to mention the easiest. Marinating it in pineapple juice begins to "cook" the salmon, and the brown sugar–spice mixture caramelizes while it finishes cooking in the oven. Salmon is so healthy, loaded with omega fatty acids. Always be sure to buy wild salmon, not farm-raised. Wild salmon is superior in flavor and texture and has less toxins than farm-raised.

4 salmon fillets, ½-pound each

2 cups pineapple juice

½ cup dark brown sugar

1 tablespoon chili powder

1½ teaspoons ground cumin

2 teaspoons ground coriander

Kosher salt and freshly ground black pepper

Place the salmon in a shallow dish. Pour pineapple juice over the fish. Cover and marinate in the refrigerator for at least 1 hour, but no more than 3 hours.

Preheat the oven to 425° F. Line a baking sheet with foil.

In a small bowl, mix together the brown sugar, chili powder, cumin, coriander, ½ teaspoon salt, and ¼ teaspoon pepper.

Remove salmon from the marinade and discard the juice. Put salmon on the baking sheet. Season the fish with salt and pepper. Evenly distribute sugar-spice mixture over the top of the fish.

Bake for 10 to 20 minutes, depending on thickness, until the fish is cooked to the desired doneness.

YIELD: 4 SERVINGS
PREP TIME: 10 MINUTES
INACTIVE PREP TIME: 1 TO 3 HOURS
COOK TIME: 10 TO 20 MINUTES

GRILLED CHIPOTLE THREE-CHEESE SANDWICH

When I was in college, I worked in a great little restaurant called Kona Bistro. Employees ate for free, and after a long shift, I always had this sandwich. Be careful, the chipotle puree is spicy!

Place the chipotle peppers and their sauce in a food processor or a blender and puree until smooth. With the machine running slowly drizzle in the olive oil. Place the chipotle puree in a small bowl and set aside. Can be stored in an airtight container in the refrigerator.

Preheat a large heavy skillet, grill pan, or griddle to medium heat.

Place the bread slices on a work surface and spread each slice with ½-1 tablespoon chipotle puree (depending on how spicy you like it). Layer half the bread slices with two slices of each cheese and a few slices of the tomatoes and onions. Top with the remaining slices of bread, chipotle side down. Spread the top and bottom of each sandwich with butter.

Grill each sandwich for 3 to 4 minutes on each side until the cheese is completely melted and the bread is golden brown. Slice the sandwiches in half and serve immediately.

YIELD: 6 SERVINGS
PREP TIME: 15 MINUTES
COOK TIME: 6 TO 8 MINUTES

One 7-ounce can chipotle peppers in adobo sauce (I like La Costena brand)

¼ cup olive oil

12 slices Monterey Jack cheese

12 slices Swiss cheese

12 slices Cheddar cheese

2 Roma tomatoes, sliced crosswise

½ red onion, very thinly sliced

12 slices sourdough bread (thickly sliced if possible)

12 tablespoons butter (1½ sticks), softened

PIZZA MARGHERITA

I'm a purist and my favorite pizza is the classic pizza Margherita. When I was in college, studying in Florence, we ate at Dante's Pizzeria almost every night. I always ordered a Margherita, and the crust was so paper thin that I would eat the entire pie on my own. Of course, I came home ten pounds heavier, but it was worth every bite!

Pizza Dough (page 159)

Pizza Sauce (recipe follows)

Cornmeal

Olive oil

Kosher salt

2 balls fresh mozzarella cheese, cut into thin slices

8 fresh basil leaves, shredded

Special equipment: **baker's peel and pizza stone (for best results) or cookie sheet**

Pizza Sauce

2 tablespoons olive oil

1 tablespoon minced fresh oregano

1 tablespoon minced fresh basil

4 very ripe Roma tomatoes, diced

¼ teaspoon kosher salt

Freshly ground black pepper

YIELD: 2 10-INCH PIZZAS
PREP TIME: 15 MINUTES
INACTIVE PREP TIME: 1½ TO 2 HOURS FOR PIZZA DOUGH
COOK TIME: 10 MINUTES

FOR THE PIZZA

Prepare the pizza dough (see page 165). Put a pizza stone on the lowest oven rack and remove all the other racks. Preheat the oven to 500° F. Let stone preheat for about 1 hour. While the stone is preheating, prepare the sauce.

Sprinkle a baker's peel with 1 tablespoon cornmeal and carefully slide dough onto the peel. Jerk the peel in a back and forth motion once or twice to be sure the dough does not stick. If the dough sticks, add extra cornmeal. Drizzle the dough with olive oil and sprinkle with salt. Spread half the pizza sauce evenly over the dough, leaving a small border.

To place the pizza on the stone, open the oven and line up the far edge of the peel with the far edge of the stone. Tilt the peel and jerk gently to start the pizza moving. When the edge of pizza touches the stone, pull back the peel in a quick motion in order to transfer the pizza to the stone. Bake for 5 minutes. With the peel rotate the pizza and top with half the mozzarella. Bake an additional 3 to 5 minutes, until the cheese is melted and the crust appears crisp and golden brown. Slide the peel under the pizza and remove from the oven. Cool slightly on a cutting surface. Scatter with half of the basil, slice, and serve. Repeat the process with the other pizza.

FOR THE PIZZA SAUCE

Place the olive oil, oregano, basil, tomatoes, and salt in a small pot over medium heat. Bring to a simmer, stirring frequently. Reduce the heat to low and cook for 10 minutes. Transfer to a food processor and puree until smooth. Season with pepper to taste. Reserve until ready to make the pizzas.

FRESH MORELS WITH APPLES AND EGG NOODLES

Every spring, when the rains come and the temperatures begin to rise, my stepfather, Jim, begins his morel hunting. Morels are rare mushrooms that look like pointy sponges. He stays secretive about his hunting spots, but he shared this recipe with me.

5 tablespoons unsalted butter

¾ pound fresh morels (I like to slice the large ones and leave the small ones whole)

½ cup minced shallots (about 3 large shallots)

2 Granny Smith apples, cored and cut into matchsticks (leave the skins on)

1 dried chipotle pepper, seeded, minced

1 tablespoon all-purpose flour

1/2 cup white wine or apple juice

1 cup low-sodium chicken or vegetable stock

½ pound fresh pencil asparagus, tips only

½ pound egg noodles, slightly undercooked and drained

1¼ teaspoons kosher salt

½ teaspoon freshly ground black pepper

½ cup loosely packed baby spinach

In a large skillet, melt the butter over medium high heat. Add the morels and shallots. Sauté about 2 minutes. Add the apples, chipotle, and flour, and sauté another 2 minutes. Add the wine and stock and bring to a boil. Add asparagus and pasta and cook until the asparagus is tender, about 3 to 5 minutes. Add the salt, pepper, and spinach. Serve immediately.

YIELD: 4 TO 6 SERVINGS
PREP TIME: 20 MINUTES
COOK TIME: 12 MINUTES

MACARONI AND FOUR CHEESES

When I was in college, I practically lived on macaroni and cheese. I hate to admit how much neon-orange powdered stuff I ate, but it was cheap and easy. Now my tastes have evolved, and I make this macaroni and four cheeses. You can use almost any combination of hard cheese that you like. I love the added kick that the crumbled blue cheese adds to the Cheddar, fontina, and Parmesan. This makes a great side dish, but also an excellent vegetarian main course when served with a couple of vegetable sides.

Preheat the oven to 375° F. Bring a large pot of salted water to a boil. Add the macaroni and cook according to package instructions. Drain well.

In a large saucepan, melt 4 tablespoons of the butter. Add the flour and cook for about 2 minutes, stirring with a whisk. While still whisking, add the milk and cook until thickened. Remove from heat and stir in Cheddar, fontina, blue cheese, salt, and pepper. Stir in macaroni. Pour into a 3-quart baking dish.

Arrange the sliced tomatoes on top. In a medium bowl melt the remaining 1 tablespoon butter and mix with the bread crumbs and Parmesan. Sprinkle the breadcrumb mixture over the tomatoes. Bake for 30 minutes, until bubbly and golden brown. Serve immediately.

YIELD: 6 TO 8 SERVINGS
PREP TIME: 20 MINUTES
COOK TIME: 45 MINUTES

1 pound macaroni (can use regular elbow macaroni or penne, farfalle, etc.)

5 tablespoons unsalted butter

¼ cup all-purpose flour

2 cups milk

1½ cups grated sharp Cheddar cheese

½ cup grated fontina cheese

½ cup crumbled blue cheese

1 teaspoon kosher salt

½ teaspoon freshly ground black pepper

4 Roma tomatoes, sliced

¼ cup dry bread crumbs

2 tablespoons grated Parmesan cheese

SIDE DISHES

Though it may sound surprising coming from a Southern cook, I was a vegetarian for many years. I often found myself eating meals composed entirely of side dishes— whether at restaurants without vegetarian options or at dinner parties. I was never bothered, though, because I love side dishes. There are so many ways to make vegetables interesting and add some color to the dinner plate. Any of these side dishes will make the perfect addition to your meal.

CREAMY MASHED POTATOES

PEAS WITH BACON AND ROASTED RED PEPPERS

ROASTED CARROTS WITH HONEY AND MINT

ROASTED CAULIFLOWER

GREEN BEAN CASSEROLE

SPINACH AND BACON TIMBALES

HASH BROWNS

BROCCOLI AND CHEESE SAUCE

SESAME CORN SAUTÉ

BARLEY PILAF

HOT AND SOUR CABBAGE

SWEET POTATO LATKES

STIR-FRIED BRUSSELS SPROUTS

VIDALIA ONION PIE

BAKED BEANS

GRILLED CORN ON THE COB

BRAISED KALE

CREAMY MASHED POTATOES

The first Thanksgiving I lived in New York, I decided to throw a dinner party for sixteen people. I was still living among boxes, and I bit off more than I could chew, so to speak. I was running around like a chicken with its head cut off when my friend Kevin jumped in and offered to make the mashed potatoes. I actually liked his method better than my own, and now I always make Kevin's mashed potatoes.

2½ pounds Yukon gold potatoes, peeled and quartered

1 tablespoon kosher salt

One 8-ounce package of cream cheese, cut into chunks

½ cup milk

4 tablespoons (½ stick) unsalted butter, melted

½ teaspoon freshly ground black pepper

Place the potatoes in a medium pot. Cover with cold water and add 1 teaspoon salt. Bring the water to a boil over medium-high heat. Lower the heat to a simmer and cook until potatoes are fork tender, about 20 minutes. Drain.

Return the potatoes to the pot and add the cream cheese, milk, butter, 2 teaspoons salt, and pepper. Using a handheld electric mixer, whip the potatoes until smooth and creamy with no lumps. Adjust the seasoning to taste.

YIELD: 6 CUPS (4 TO 6 SERVINGS)
PREP TIME: 20 MINUTES
COOK TIME: 20 MINUTES

ROASTED CAULIFLOWER

Cauliflower is one of those vegetables that can be kind of boring on its own, but with a little help, it can have its own pizzazz. The garlic, lemon juice, capers, and red pepper give this recipe a decidedly Mediterranean flair. I usually serve it alongside a roasted fish.

1 medium head of cauliflower, cut into bite-size florets (about 5 cups)

¼ cup olive oil

1 garlic clove, thinly sliced

1 tablespoon fresh lemon juice

1 tablespoon capers, rinsed and drained

¾ teaspoon kosher salt

¼ teaspoon freshly ground black pepper

¼ teaspoon red pepper flakes

¼ cup grated Parmesan cheese

Preheat oven to 450° F.

In a small bowl, combine the olive oil, garlic, lemon juice, capers, salt, pepper, and red pepper.

Place cauliflower in a roasting pan and mix with the olive oil mixture. Roast for 15 to 20 minutes, stirring occasionally. Remove from oven and top with Parmesan. Roast an additional 1 to 2 minutes, until cheese is melted.

YIELD: 4 SERVINGS
PREP TIME: 10 MINUTES
COOK TIME: 20 MINUTES

GREEN BEAN CASSEROLE

At every potluck dinner, it seems like someone shows up with a green bean casserole. To be honest, I never really cared for the traditional preparation with canned cream of mushroom soup and canned fried onions. I always thought it was gloppy and greasy. I tried recreating it by making a homemade cream sauce, using fresh green beans and mushrooms, and fried shallots. Now I am a convert—I love this version of the classic.

Preheat the oven to 375° F. Butter a 13 by 9-inch baking dish. Bring a large pot of salted water to a boil over high heat. Cook the green beans just until tender, about 5 minutes. Drain and set aside in a large bowl.

Meanwhile, melt the butter in a large skillet over medium heat. Add the onions and cook until translucent, about 4 minutes. Add the mushrooms and cook until most of their liquid has evaporated, about 8 minutes. Reduce heat to medium-low and stir in 3 tablespoons flour. Cook until golden brown, about 4 minutes. Add the milk, slowly at first, stirring constantly with a wooden spoon until the milk has incorporated. Continue stirring occasionally until the mixture has thickened, making sure to scrape all over the bottom of the pan. Stir in 2 teaspoons salt, the pepper, and hot sauce to taste. Pour the mushroom mixture over beans and toss to combine. Stir in the Parmesan.

Pour bean mixture into the baking dish. Sprinkle the bread crumbs on top. Bake until the breadcrumbs are golden, about 10 minutes.

While the casserole is baking. Heat about 1 inch of canola oil in a skillet over medium-high heat. Toss shallots in 2 tablespoons flour. Fry the shallots until golden brown. Drain on a paper towel and sprinkle with salt. Top the casserole with fried shallots.

YIELD: 6 TO 8 SERVINGS
PREP TIME: 15 MINUTES
COOK TIME: 30 MINUTES

1½ pounds green beans, trimmed and cut in into bite-size pieces

4 tablespoons (½ stick) unsalted butter

1 medium yellow onion, finely diced

1 pound white button mushrooms, sliced

5 tablespoons all-purpose flour

2 cups milk

Kosher salt

1 teaspoon freshly ground black pepper

Hot sauce, like Tabasco

1 cup grated Parmesan cheese

¼ cup dry bread crumbs

6 shallots, thinly sliced

2 to 4 cups canola oil

BROCCOLI AND CHEESE SAUCE

My mom never had any trouble getting me to eat my vegetables when I was a kid. In fact, at family dinners, my cousins used to slip me their vegetables so that they wouldn't get in trouble for not finishing their plates. But whenever broccoli and cheese was on the menu, I only got a single serving.

Melt the butter in a medium saucepan over medium heat. Add the flour and cook, stirring constantly, until the flour turns light gold, about 2 minutes. Stir in the paprika and cook 1 minute more. Reduce the heat to low and slowly add 1 cup milk, stirring constantly. Bring to a low boil. When the sauce begins to thicken, add the cheese and stir until the cheese has melted. Stir in the salt, pepper, cayenne (if using), and up to ¼ cup milk to achieve desired consistency.

Meanwhile, place the broccoli in a steamer over high heat. Cook until tender, about 5 minutes.

Serve the broccoli with the cheese sauce drizzled over the top or in a serving bowl alongside.

2 tablespoons (¼ stick) unsalted butter

2 tablespoons all-purpose flour

½ teaspoon paprika

1 to 1¼ cups milk

2 cups shredded Cheddar cheese

¼ teaspoon kosher salt

⅛ teaspoon freshly ground black pepper

Pinch of cayenne, optional

2 bunches of broccoli, florets only

Monterey Jack cheese or Swiss cheese can be substituted for the Cheddar cheese. If using a white cheese, omit the paprika and use white pepper instead of black pepper, if possible.

YIELD: 4 TO 6 SERVINGS
PREP TIME: 5 MINUTES
COOK TIME: 10 MINUTES

SESAME CORN SAUTÉ

There is nothing that I love in the summertime more than fresh sweet corn. When I moved to New York, I discovered Long Island corn, the sweetest I have ever tasted. I usually just steam it and eat it straight from the cob, but when I'm having company I like to cut it off the cob to make it easier for everyone to eat. I use fresh basil in this recipe, but sometimes I substitute with cilantro and a squeeze of lime juice.

2½ teaspoons sesame seeds

3 tablespoons olive oil

1 garlic clove, minced

6 ears fresh corn, shucked, kernals cut off the cob (about 4 cups)

½ teaspoon kosher salt

⅛ teaspoon freshly ground black pepper

2 tablespoons fresh basil chiffonade (very thinly sliced)

Preheat oven to 350° F. Toast the sesame seeds on a baking sheet until very light tan, about 6 minutes. Remove from the oven and set aside.

In a large skillet over medium heat, heat olive oil and sauté garlic for about 2 minutes. Add the corn, salt, and pepper. Cook until corn is just tender, about 8 minutes. Gently toss in the sesame seeds and basil.

YIELD: 4 TO 6 SERVINGS
PREP TIME: 10 MINUTES
COOK TIME: 15 MINUTES

BARLEY PILAF

I'm always looking for a starch alternative to rice. I love the texture of barley, and it looks so attractive when mixed with the bright colors of vegetables and cranberries. It pairs nicely with simple grilled chicken or fish.

3 cups low-sodium chicken broth

1 cup pearl barley

2 tablespoons fresh lemon juice

2 tablespoons olive oil

½ cup finely chopped yellow onion

1 garlic clove, minced

½ cup frozen peas, thawed

½ cup finely diced carrots

¼ cup dried cranberries

2 tablespoons chopped fresh flat-leaf parsley

¾ teaspoon kosher salt

¼ teaspoon freshly ground black pepper

Bring broth and lemon juice to a boil in a medium saucepan over high heat. Stir in the barley and reduce the heat to a simmer. Cover and cook until tender, 25 to 30 minutes.

While the barley is cooking, heat the oil in a medium sauté pan over medium-high heat. Add the onions, garlic, and carrots. Cook until the onions are translucent and carrots are tender, 10 to 12 minutes. Stir in the peas and cook until heated through. Add the cooked barley and stir in cranberries, parsley, salt, and pepper. Transfer to a serving bowl and serve.

YIELD: 4 SERVINGS
PREP TIME: 10 MINUTES
COOK TIME: 30 MINUTES

HOT AND SOUR CABBAGE

Hot and sour cabbage is a favorite of many, but did you know there is actually a scientific reason for combining red cabbage and vinegar? In a food science class I took during college, we did a cooking experiment with red cabbage. If cooked without the acid of vinegar, it turns a deep teal color. Strange, but true!

Place the bacon in a large skillet over medium heat. Cook until crispy and the fat is rendered, about 8 to 10 minutes. Using a slotted spoon, remove the bacon pieces and reserve, leaving the grease in the pan. Add the onion and sauté until translucent, about 4 minutes. Add the cabbage, wine, vinegar, and sugar. Stir to combine. Cover and let cook about 10 minutes, stirring occasionally. Add the salt and pepper. Cook another 10 to 15 minutes, until the cabbage is tender. Remove from heat and add the reserved bacon. Transfer to a platter and serve immediately.

YIELD: 6 SERVINGS
PREP TIME: 15 MINUTES
COOK TIME: 30 MINUTES

3 slices thick-cut bacon, chopped

1 medium yellow onion, diced (about 1 cup)

1 small head of red cabbage (about 2 pounds), cored, quartered, and chopped into 1-inch pieces

1 cup red wine

¾ cup red wine vinegar

¼ cup light brown sugar, lightly packed

1½ teaspoons kosher salt

½ teaspoon freshly ground black pepper

SWEET POTATO LATKES

My stepfather makes these sweet potato latkes and serves them with his mother Viola's famous homemade applesauce. She lives far away, but every fall she sends him some applesauce and he whips up a batch of these latkes. My mom and I eat them as fast as he can fry them!

Press out the excess water from the grated potatoes and sweet potatoes. You should be left with about two cups of potatoes. In a medium bowl, mix the potatoes with the leeks, eggs, bread crumbs, salt, and pepper.

In a large heavy skillet (preferably cast-iron) over medium-high heat, melt butter with the oil. Use a large spoon to drop the potato batter into the skillet. Flatten the potatoes to about 3 inches in diameter. Fry the pancakes until golden brown, 4 to 5 minutes on each side. Drain the pancakes on paper towels and serve with sour cream, apple sauce, and cherries on the side.

YIELD: 4 SIDE SERVINGS
PREP TIME: 15 MINUTES
COOK TIME: 20 MINUTES

2 medium Idaho potatoes, peeled and grated

1 medium sweet potato, peeled and grated

¼ cup finely diced leeks, white part only

2 large eggs, lightly beaten

¼ cup dry bread crumbs

1 teaspoon kosher salt

½ teaspoon freshly ground black pepper

3 tablespoons unsalted butter

¼ cup vegetable oil

Sour cream, applesauce, and sour cherries (I like to rehydrate dried cherries)

STIR-FRIED BRUSSELS SPROUTS

Brussels sprouts have a bad rep. After childhood encounters with mushy, overcooked brussels sprouts, it doesn't surprise me that most people don't like them. They happen to be my husband's favorite vegetable, so I'm always coming up with different recipes. This is one of our favorites.

1 tablespoon vegetable oil

⅓ cup chopped scallions (about 4 scallions), cut on the diagonal

½ teaspoon peeled and grated fresh ginger

¼ cup slivered almonds

1 pound brussels sprouts, trimmed and quartered

⅔ cup vegetable or low-sodium chicken stock

1 teaspoon kosher salt

½ teaspoon freshly ground black pepper

Heat the vegetable oil over medium heat in a wok or large skillet. Add the scallions, ginger, and almonds, and stir-fry until almonds begin to brown, 3 to 4 minutes. Add the brussels sprouts and stir-fry another 3 to 4 minutes. Add the stock and cook uncovered for about 6 minutes, or until the sprouts are tender and almost all the liquid has evaporated. Season with salt and pepper, and serve immediately.

YIELD: 4 TO 6 SERVINGS
PREP TIME: 15 MINUTES
COOK TIME: 15 MINUTES

VIDALIA ONION PIE

I love the flavor of onions after they have cooked for a long period of time. For this onion pie, I first sauté the onions until tender and then finish cooking them in the oven. Their sweetness, combined with the salty cracker crust and the sharp Cheddar cheese flavor, makes for a real palate pleaser. This pie is great to bring as a side dish to a potluck dinner because it still tastes delicious at room temperature. Since it has a custard base, I sometimes even serve it at brunch. If you don't have access to Vidalia onions, substitute your favorite.

1 sleeve of Ritz crackers (about 35 crackers)

4 tablespoons (½ stick) unsalted butter, melted

1 large Vidalia onion, thinly sliced (about 2½ cups)

1 garlic clove, minced

2 tablespoons olive oil

2 large eggs

½ cup milk

½ teaspoon kosher salt

¼ teaspoon freshly ground black pepper

¼ cup shredded sharp Cheddar cheese

Preheat oven to 350° F.

Place the crackers in a food processor and pulse until finely ground. Combine the cracker crumbs and the melted butter. Press into a 9-inch pie plate to form a crust. Refrigerate for 40 minutes.

Meanwhile, sauté the onions and garlic in olive oil in a medium skillet over medium heat, until tender.

When the crust is cold, place the onions in the crust. Combine the eggs, milk, salt, and pepper. Mix well and pour over the onions. Top with the cheese.

Bake for 45 minutes, or until a knife inserted in the center comes out clean. Let the pie rest for 10 minutes before slicing and serving.

YIELD: 4 TO 6 SERVINGS
PREP TIME: 15 MINUTES
INACTIVE PREP TIME: 40 MINUTES
COOK TIME: 45 MINUTES

OUR OWN
SWEET
CORN
$.50/EAR

BREADS

Beware, low-carb dieters. . . .

There is absolutely no better scent than that of freshly baked bread. I go crazy for it! Baking bread sounds intimidating, but it's really quite easy, albeit a rather lengthy process. If you are making a yeast bread, start the dough first, and while it rises, work on the other components of your meal or do chores around the house.

Homemade breads make great gifts as well. Wrap quick breads or muffins in airtight plastic wrap and tie with a colorful ribbon for a gift that's sure to be much appreciated.

Breads

PAT'S REFRIGERATOR ROLLS

CINNAMON ROLLS

SPICY ZUCCHINI-PINEAPPLE BREAD

NUTTY BANANA BREAD

PIZZA DOUGH

MONKEY BREAD

DILL BREAD

MY CORNBREAD

MEXICAN CORNBREAD

ORANGE BLOSSOM WATER BRIOCHE

PUMPKIN MUFFINS

PAT'S REFRIGERATOR ROLLS

My great-aunt Pat is famous for her hot rolls. She has many specialties, but these rolls are my favorite. These rolls are a staple at all of our family functions. Big and fluffy in texture and fragrant with the sweet smell of yeast, these rolls just can't be beat. They usually disappear straight out of the oven.

¼ cup warm water, about 110° F

Two ¼-ounce packets active dry yeast (4 ½ teaspoons)

1 cup plus 1 teaspoon sugar

2 large eggs, lightly beaten

½ cup canola oil

1 tablespoon kosher salt

1 cup cold water

1 cup boiling water

7 to 8 cups all-purpose flour

YIELD: 24 ROLLS

PREP TIME: 45 MINUTES

INACTIVE PREP TIME: AT LEAST 6 HOURS

COOK TIME: 15 MINUTES

In a small bowl, mix the warm water with the yeast and 1 teaspoon sugar. Set aside for about 5 minutes, until the mixture starts to thicken and bubble slightly. (If the mixture does not start to bubble, the yeast is not working. Check the expiration date on the yeast and start over.)

In a large bowl, stir together 1 cup sugar, the eggs, oil, and salt. Mix in the cold water and then the boiling water. Add the yeast mixture and stir until well blended. With a wooden spoon, slowly stir in 7 cups flour, until incorporated.

Turn the dough out onto a floured surface. Coat the palms of your hands with flour and knead the dough for 8 to 10 minutes. If dough remains sticky, add an extra 1 cup or more of flour as needed. When you're done, the dough should be stretchy like elastic. Put the dough into a clean large bowl. Cover with plastic wrap and refrigerate for 3 hours.

Punch down the dough. (At this point the dough can be re-covered with plastic wrap and stored in the refrigerator for up to 24 hours. Remove the dough and continue with the recipe 3½ hours before you are ready to bake.)

Grease two 12-cup muffin tins. Place the dough on a lightly floured work surface. Using a large knife, cut the dough into 24 equal pieces. Divide each piece into three 1-inch balls. Place each set of three balls into one muffin-tin cup. Loosely cover and allow the rolls to rise for about 3 hours at room temperature.

Thirty minutes before baking, preheat the oven to 350° F.

Bake for 15 minutes, or until golden on top. Remove from the tins and serve warm.

CINNAMON ROLLS

Is there anything better than a big, hot, gooey, sticky cinnamon roll? I think not. When my grandmother made these, we would all fight over who got the center roll because it usually had the most icing. She made her icing with just confectioners' sugar and milk, but sometimes I substitute orange juice to change it up a bit.

In a small bowl, mix the warm water with the yeast and 1 teaspoon sugar. Set aside for about 5 minutes, until the mixture starts to thicken and bubble slightly. (If the mixture does not start to bubble, the yeast is not working. Check the expiration date on the yeast and start over.)

In a large bowl, stir together ½ cup sugar, the egg, oil, and salt. Mix in the cold water and then the boiling water. Add the yeast mixture and stir until well blended. With a wooden spoon, slowly stir in 4 cups flour, until incorporated.

Turn the dough out onto a floured surface. Coat the palms of your hands with flour and knead the dough for 8 to 10 minutes. If dough remains sticky, add an extra ½ cup or more of flour as needed. When you're done, the dough should be stretchy, like elastic. Put the dough into a clean large bowl. Cover with plastic wrap and refrigerate until doubled in size, about 3 hours.

Meanwhile, combine the remaining ½ cup sugar with the cinnamon in a small bowl. Grease a 13 by 9-inch baking dish with about 1 tablespoon of the melted butter, using a pastry brush.

Punch down the dough and place it on a lightly floured surface. Using a rolling pin, roll it into a rectangle about 20 by 10 inches, with the long edge facing you. Using the pastry brush, spread ¼ cup of the melted butter over the top of the dough. Sprinkle the cinnamon-sugar mixture evenly over the dough. Roll up the dough, starting with the long edge facing you, into a tight cylinder. Gently squeeze all seams and ends of the cylinder to seal it. Use a sharp knife to cut the dough into 12 even rounds. Place the rounds, cut side down, into the prepared baking dish. There will be some space in between the rounds. Brush the tops of the rolls with the remaining 1 tablespoon melted butter. Cover the dish tightly with plastic wrap and allow the dough to rise in a warm place for about 1½ to 2 hours.

Preheat the oven to 350° F. Bake the rolls until golden, 40 to 45 minutes. Meanwhile, mix the confectioners' sugar with the milk in a small bowl. When the rolls come out of the oven drizzle the icing over the hot rolls. Serve warm.

For the cinnamon rolls

¼ cup warm water, 110° F

One 1¼-ounce packet active dry yeast (2¼ teaspoons)

1 cup plus 1 teaspoon sugar

1 large egg, lightly beaten

¼ cup canola oil

2 teaspoons kosher salt

½ cup cold water

½ cup boiling water

4 to 5 cups all-purpose flour

2 tablespoons ground cinnamon

6 tablespoons (¾ stick) unsalted butter, melted

For the icing

1 cup confectioners' sugar

2 tablespoons milk or orange juice

YIELD: 12 ROLLS
PREP TIME: 20 MINUTES
INACTIVE PREP TIME:
5 HOURS
COOK TIME: 40 MINUTES

PIZZA DOUGH

My mother and I are very competitive when it comes to our pizza making. While she may think she makes the best crust, I know that I do. About eight years ago we made my stepfather do a blind taste test, and he picked me as the winner. My mother still hasn't lived it down. I think pizzas are great for a Friday night with your family. Make enough dough to let everyone create their own pizzas, and then they can sample one another's creations.

Fill a small bowl with hot tap water. Let the bowl sit for 2 minutes. Dump the water and in the bowl, combine the yeast, 1 tablespoon flour, the sugar, and ¼ cup of the warm water. Let stand for about 5 minutes. The mixture will be creamy, pastelike, and slightly bubbly. If it isn't, start over with fresh new yeast.

In a large glass or ceramic bowl, mix 2½ cups flour and the salt. Make a well in the center and with a wooden spoon, stir in the yeast mixture, 1 tablespoon oil, and remaining ¾ cup warm water. Mix until dough starts to come away from the sides of the bowl. It will be sticky.

Turn out the dough onto a lightly floured surface. Coat the palms of your hands with flour and knead for about 8 minutes. The dough will be soft and elastic. Form into a ball.

Pour the remaining 1 teaspoon olive oil into a clean large glass or ceramic bowl. Place the dough ball in the bowl and roll it around to coat all the sides with the oil. Tightly seal the bowl with plastic wrap. Set aside in a warm place away from any drafts. Allow the dough to rise until it doubles in size, 1 to 1½ hours.

After the dough rises, do not punch down. Carefully place the dough on a floured work surface. Use your fingertips to gently flatten into a disc and cut in half. Use a lightly floured rolling pin to roll each piece into a circle about 10 inches in diameter, or to desired thickness. (I like mine paper thin.) Pinch the edge to form a crust. (See page 116, Pizza Margherita, for baking instructions.)

YIELD: TWO 10-INCH PIZZAS
PREP TIME: 15 MINUTES
INACTIVE PREP TIME: 1 TO 1½ HOURS

One ¼-ounce packet active dry yeast (2¼ teaspoons)

About 3 cups all-purpose flour

1 teaspoon sugar

1 cup warm water (105° to 115° F)

2 teaspoons kosher salt

1 tablespoon plus 1 teaspoon olive oil

MONKEY BREAD

When I was in high school, I looked forward to sleepovers at my friend Erica's house because her mom always made this monkey bread. We would stay up all night eating it and gossiping about boys. Today, I like making it for breakfast when I have houseguests—we all sit around eating it in the morning as we drink our coffee.

Four 12-ounce cans regular-size flaky biscuits (such as Pillsbury)

1 cup sugar

2 tablespoons ground cinnamon

4 tablespoons (½ stick) unsalted butter

1 teaspoon pure vanilla extract

Preheat oven to 350° F. Grease a 10-inch Bundt or tube pan.

Cut biscuits into quarters and roll into balls. Combine the ⅔ cup sugar and 1 tablespoon cinnamon in a shallow dish. Roll the biscuit balls in the cinnamon-sugar. Place the coated balls in the pan, sprinkling some of the cinnamon-sugar over the balls occasionally while filling the pan.

Melt the butter in a small saucepan over medium-low heat. Add the remaining ⅓ cup sugar, 1 tablespoon cinnamon, and the vanilla. Warm, stirring occasionally, until the sugar dissolves. Pour over the top of the biscuit balls. Bake for 30 minutes, or until the top of the bread is golden and caramelized. Remove from the oven and let sit at least 5 minutes. Unmold the Monkey Bread onto a cake plate. Slice or pull apart to serve.

YIELD: 12 SERVINGS
PREP TIME: 20 MINUTES
COOK TIME: 30 MINUTES

MEXICAN CORNBREAD

I don't know why this recipe is called "Mexican." I'm pretty sure it isn't served anywhere in Mexico, but that's just what we always called this cornbread. The red pepper flakes pack some heat, and the corn provides a little sugar burst. The intense flavors sure do please the palate.

3 cups cornmeal

2 tablespoons baking powder

2 tablespoons sugar

1 tablespoon red pepper flakes

2½ teaspoons kosher salt

2 cups milk

½ cup canola oil

One 14.75-ounce can cream-style corn

1 cup grated sharp Cheddar cheese

1 cup finely diced yellow onion (about 1 small onion)

½ cup diced green bell pepper

Preheat oven to 375° F. Grease a 13 by 9 by 2-inch baking dish and place in the oven to heat while you make the batter.

In a large bowl, combine the cornmeal, baking powder, sugar, red pepper flakes, and salt. Stir to combine. Add milk, oil, and cream-style corn and stir until just combined. Stir in the onion, green pepper, and cheese just until incorporated.

Carefully remove the hot baking dish from the oven and pour the batter into it. Return to the oven and bake for 45 minutes, or until a toothpick comes out clean. Let cool for 5 minutes. Cut into squares and serve.

YIELD: 12 TO 16 SERVINGS
PREP TIME: 10 MINUTES
COOK TIME: 45 MINUTES

ORANGE BLOSSOM WATER BRIOCHE

My friend Ahmad and I took a baking class together last year, and we were so excited to learn all of our favorite French pastries. Having grown up in the Middle East and Paris, he loves the flavors of orange blossom water, which happened to be the favorite flavoring of Marie Antoinette. So if you are in the mood to pamper your taste buds like a French royal, indulge in these brioche.

In a small saucepan, heat the milk and 1 tablespoon sugar over low heat just until warmed (about 110° F), about 2 minutes. Sprinkle with the yeast and let sit 2 minutes. Gently stir and let sit until the mixture is foamy, 5 to 7 minutes more. (If the mixture doesn't foam, start again with new yeast, milk, and sugar.)

In the bowl of an electric mixer, using the paddle attachment, combine 5 of the eggs, the remaining ⅓ cup sugar, the orange blossom water, and salt. Mix on low until the ingredients are mixed. Add 2 cups flour and mix for about 2 minutes, until all of the ingredients are wet. Add the yeast mixture and 2 more cups flour and mix for about 3 to 4 minutes, until all the ingredients are combined and the dough is very stretchy, like elastic. It should be yellow, smooth, and soft. Add the butter, a few cubes at a time with the machine running. Add the remaining ½ cup flour as the last of the butter is being added. Continue mixing, adding more flour if necessary, until the dough is soft (scrape the dough off the paddle and sides of the bowl a couple of times during the mixing). Change to the dough hook attachment and knead the dough until it forms a smooth ball, 7 to 10 minutes

Lightly oil a large bowl. Put in the dough, cover with plastic wrap, and set aside in a warm place away from drafts to rise until doubled in size, about 2 hours. Punch down the dough, re-cover, and place in the refrigerator for at least 4 hours and up to overnight.

Grease two 9 by 5 by 3-inch loaf pans. Remove the dough from the refrigerator. Sprinkle a work surface with flour and coat your palms. Divide the dough in half. Gently knead each dough ball into a log about 9 inches long. Place the dough logs in the loaf pans. Cover with plastic wrap and allow the dough to rise until doubled in sized, 1 to 2 hours.

Preheat the oven to 350° F. Lightly beat the remaining egg. Brush the tops of the loaves with the egg and bake until deep golden brown, 35 to 45 minutes. Remove from pans and cool completely on a wire rack.

¼ cup milk

⅓ cup plus 1 tablespoon sugar

One ¼ ounce packet active dry yeast (2¼ teaspoons)

6 large eggs

2 tablespoons orange blossom water (can be found in gourmet specialty stores)

2 teaspoons kosher salt

4½ cups bread flour, plus more if necessary

½ pound (2 sticks) cold unsalted butter, cut into cubes

YIELD: 10 TO 12 SERVINGS
PREP TIME: 30 MINUTES
INACTIVE PREP TIME: 14 HOURS
COOK TIME: 35 MINUTES

PUMPKIN MUFFINS

When the leaves start to turn and the crisp breezes of autumn start to blow, one of the first things I think about is this recipe for pumpkin muffins. They are great to serve with Sunday brunch and the leftovers are great eaten throughout the week lightly toasted and spread with cream cheese.

Preheat oven to 350° F. Grease a 12-cup muffin tin.

In a small bowl, mix together the flour, baking soda, cinnamon, nutmeg, and salt.

In a medium bowl, beat together the sugar, oil, eggs, and vanilla. Add the pumpkin puree and mix well. Add the dry ingredients and stir until just combined.

Pour the batter into the muffin tin. Bake for 20 minutes, or until a toothpick comes out clean. Let the muffin tin cool on a wire rack for 10 minutes. Remove the muffins.

YIELD: 12 MUFFINS
PREP TIME: 10 MINUTES
COOK TIME: 20 MINUTES

2 cups all-purpose flour

2 teaspoons baking soda

1 teaspoon ground cinnamon

½ teaspoon freshly grated nutmeg

½ teaspoon kosher salt

2 cups sugar

½ cup canola oil

2 large eggs, lightly beaten

1 teaspoon pure vanilla extract

One 15-ounce can pure pumpkin puree (not pie filling)

BREAKFASTS

Breakfast, the most important meal of the day . . .

When I was growing up, we always had a big breakfast, usually pancakes, biscuits and gravy, bacon and eggs, or homemade cinnamon rolls. Breakfast wasn't just about fueling up for the day; it was a real bonding time for all of us. We started out together with laughter, and it always made for a more relaxing day overall.

Nowadays, like most people, I have my breakfast on the go as I rush out the door. On the weekends, though, I like to take time to follow my family's tradition and make a big breakfast. I invite friends over, and as we drink our coffee, we go over the events of the previous week.

BIG BATCH OF GRANDMA'S BISCUITS

When I was growing up, Grandma used to make these every Saturday morning for breakfast. Grandpa and I usually behaved as though we were in an eating contest, polishing off at least three or four each. One with butter, another with strawberry jam, one dipped in molasses, and another smothered in sausage gravy. These biscuits might as well spell W-E-E-K-E-N-D-S.

Preheat oven to 450° F. Grease a baking sheet.

In a large mixing bowl, combine 2½ cups flour and the butter. Using a pastry blender, cut the butter into the flour until it resembles coarse meal. Stir in the baking powder, baking soda, salt, and sugar. Make a well in the center and pour in the buttermilk. Mix with a fork until all of the ingredients are incorporated and the dough begins to shape into a ball. (The dough will be slightly dry.)

Sprinkle a work surface with flour, coat your palms, and rub some on a rolling pin. Turn out the dough onto the work surface. Knead the dough for 1 to 2 minutes, folding it over onto itself each time. Roll the dough to about ½-inch thick. Flour a 3-inch biscuit cutter (or the rim of a glass) and cut out the biscuits. Reshape the leftover dough into a ball, roll it out again, and cut out more biscuits until there is no dough remaining.

Place the biscuits on the baking sheet and bake for 10 to 12 minutes, until the tops are golden brown. While the biscuits are still hot, spread some softened butter on top of each one with a pastry brush and let it melt.

YIELD: 12 TO 15 BISCUITS
PREP TIME: 20 MINUTES
COOK TIME: 10 TO 12 MINUTES

2½ to 3 cups all-purpose flour

8 tablespoons (1 stick) unsalted butter, chilled and cut into cubes (I like using Smart Balance spread. It gives the same texture as shortening.)

1 tablespoon baking powder

¼ teaspoon baking soda

1 teaspoon kosher salt

1 teaspoon sugar

1 cup buttermilk

4 tablespoons (½ stick) unsalted butter, softened

Sausage Gravy, optional (recipe follows, on page 176)

Special equipment: 3-inch biscuit cutter and pastry blender

SAUSAGE GRAVY

When I make biscuits, I usually make this sausage gravy. I love to split open a hot biscuit and smother it with gravy. It is so creamy and rich with just the right amount of spice from the breakfast sausage. This certainly makes for a hearty breakfast.

1 pound breakfast sausage, bulk

Unsalted butter, optional

3 tablespoons all-purpose flour

2 cups milk

1 teaspoon kosher salt

½ teaspoon freshly ground black pepper

In a large skillet, cook the sausage over medium heat, breaking it up with a wooden spoon into crumbles. Using a slotted spoon, transfer the sausage to a side dish and reserve. Pour out all but ¼ cup fat. (If you have less than ¼ cup fat, add butter to make up the difference.) Stir in the flour and cook about 2 minutes over medium-low heat. Whisk in the milk and cook until the sauce begins to thicken, but do not boil. Stir in the reserved sausage and the salt and pepper. Serve with buttermilk biscuits.

YIELD: 4 SERVINGS
COOK TIME: 15 MINUTES

SOUFFLÉD PUMPKIN PANCAKE

I created this recipe one fall weekend morning when I was in the mood for something with pumpkin. I was almost out of flour, so pumpkin muffins were out of the question. This little experiment turned out to be fabulously light and delicious.

Preheat the oven to 375° F.

Melt the butter in a 10-inch skillet over medium-low heat. Pour 3 tablespoons of the butter into a medium bowl and set aside. Add the brown sugar to the remaining butter in the skillet. Stir until the sugar begins to melt. Add the pecans and cook for 2 minutes. Transfer the pecans to a small dish and set aside. Reserve the skillet for the pancake.

In a small bowl mix together the flour, pumpkin pie spice, and salt.

Add the egg yolks, buttermilk, and vanilla to the reserved melted butter and whisk until blended. Gradually whisk in the flour. Stir in the pumpkin puree. Set aside.

In a very clean bowl, using a handheld electric mixer, whip the egg whites until frothy. Gradually add the granulated sugar and beat until stiff peaks form. Gently fold the egg whites into the pumpkin batter. Carefully spoon the batter into the skillet. Sprinkle the top with the reserved pecans. Bake for 25 to 30 minutes, until golden brown.

Dust the pancake with confectioners' sugar. Cut into wedges and serve with maple syrup.

YIELD: 4 TO 6 SERVINGS
PREP TIME: 20 MINUTES
COOK TIME: 30 MINUTES

4 tablespoons (½ stick) unsalted butter

1 tablespoon dark brown sugar

¼ cup pecan halves

⅔ cup all-purpose flour

1 teaspoon pumpkin pie spice

¼ teaspoon kosher salt

4 large eggs, separated

⅔ cup buttermilk

1¼ teaspoons pure vanilla extract

1 cup pure pumpkin puree (homemade or storebought)

⅓ cup granulated sugar

Confectioners' sugar

Pure maple syrup

BROWN-SUGAR BACON

Fact: Bacon makes everything taste better. And this recipe actually makes *bacon* taste even better. The sugar caramelizes on the bacon and the mustard adds just a little kick. Serve it for breakfast, or after cooking break it into 1-inch pieces for a cocktail-party snack.

1 pound applewood-smoked bacon

½ cup packed dark brown sugar

1 tablespoon Dijon mustard

Preheat the oven to 400° F. Line a rimmed baking sheet with aluminum foil or parchment paper. Place a wire cooling rack on top.

In a medium bowl, combine the brown sugar and mustard. Add the bacon and toss to coat. Lay out the bacon slices flat on the rack. Brush with any remaining sugar. Roast the bacon for 25 to 30 minutes. Let drain on the rack for a few minutes before serving. Serve whole or cut into 1-inch pieces.

YIELD: 4 TO 6 SERVINGS
PREP TIME: 10 MINUTES
COOK TIME: 25 MINUTES

TROPICAL FRUIT SMOOTHIE

Anyone who says they don't have time for breakfast should try my smoothie recipe. Whenever I am in a hurry, I make one of these, put it in a to-go cup, and I'm out the door. The tofu gives you a serving of protein in the morning and it does not affect the flavor. You can buy frozen fruits in the freezer department and they are usually cheaper than out-of-season fresh. If I see that any of my fresh fruit is ripening before I can eat it, I chop it up and freeze it for smoothies.

1 cup soy milk or skim milk

⅓ cup firm tofu, roughly chopped (about 2½ ounces)

¼ cup frozen papaya, roughly chopped

¼ cup frozen pineapple, roughly chopped

¼ cup frozen mango, roughly chopped

1 tablespoon honey or more to taste

¼ teaspoon pure vanilla extract

Place all the ingredients in a blender. Blend, pulsing the machine if necessary, until smooth, making sure the honey is dissolved. Serve immediately.

YIELD: 1¾ CUPS (1 TO 2 SERVINGS)
PREP TIME: 5 MINUTES

BERRY MILK WITH CEREAL

My friend Jane told me how to make this berry milk. Starting the day with two cups of berries provides a powerful punch of antioxidants. Blending the berries with only one cup of milk creates a thick and creamy concoction that is so satisfying poured over bran cereal.

Blend the milk, raspberries, and blueberries in a blender until smooth. Pour over the cereal.

YIELD: 1 SERVING
PREP TIME: 3 MINUTES

1 cup skim milk

1 cup fresh raspberries

1 cup fresh blueberries

1 cup bran cereal

HEALTHY GRANOLA

I love granola, but I hate the fact that it's so darn fattening when it tastes like it should be healthy! My mom and I came up with this recipe and I love it. I promise you won't miss all the butter.

Preheat oven to 350° F.

In a large bowl, mix together the oats, sunflower and pumpkin seeds, coconut, wheat germ, nuts, cinnamon, and salt.

In a small saucepan melt butter in the maple syrup over low heat. Stir in the vanilla. Add to the oat mixture. Add 2 tablespoons water and stir until well combined. Spread the granola evenly on a large baking sheet. Bake for 30 minutes, stirring at 10-minute intervals to ensure uniform baking, until golden brown. Remove from oven and cool in the pan. Stir in the dried fruits.

> When completely cooled, place in an airtight container. Granola will keep at room temperature for 1 to 2 weeks. It also freezes well for future use.

YIELD: 8 CUPS (10-12 SERVINGS)
PREP TIME: 10 MINUTES
COOK TIME: 30 MINUTES

3 cups rolled oats

½ cup unsalted hulled sunflower seeds

½ cup unsalted hulled pumpkin seeds

½ cup flaked coconut

¼ cup wheat germ

1½ cups chopped unsalted mixed nuts (almonds, pecans, walnuts, Brazil nuts, cashews, etc.)

1 teaspoon ground cinnamon

½ teaspoon kosher salt

4 tablespoons (½ stick) unsalted butter or canola oil

⅓ cup pure maple syrup

1 teaspoon pure vanilla extract

1 cup chopped mixed dried fruit (raisins, cranberries, dates, apricots, figs, prunes, etc.)

FRUIT SALAD WITH CUSTARD SAUCE

Whenever I am having houseguests, I like to make a fruit salad for breakfast ahead of time and store it in the refrigerator. Everyone loves starting their day with the fresh flavors and beautiful bright colors. The custard sauce can also be made ahead of time—it adds such a nice, elegant touch.

For the fruit salad

1 medium pineapple, peeled, cored, and cut into chunks (about 3 cups)

1 seedless orange, peeled and cut into chunks (about 1 cup)

1 medium apple, cored and cut into chunks (about 1 cup)

½ cantaloupe, peeled, seeded, and cut into chunks (about 2 cups)

½ honeydew, peeled, seeded, and cut into chunks (about 3 cups)

1 cup strawberries, stems removed and sliced in half

2 kiwi fruit, peeled and cut into chunks (about ½ cup)

1 cup blueberries

2 tablespoons finely chopped fresh mint

¼ cup fresh lime juice

¼ cup superfine sugar

For the custard

2 cups milk

1 whole vanilla bean

4 egg yolks, lightly beaten

¼ cup granulated sugar

⅛ teaspoon freshly grated nutmeg

FOR THE FRUIT SALAD

In a large bowl, toss together all ingredients. Cover and refrigerate until ready to serve.

FOR THE CUSTARD

Prepare an ice bath.

Place the milk in the metal top of a double boiler over 1 inch water. Slice open the vanilla bean lengthwise, scrape the beans into the milk, and discard pod. Stir to combine. Heat the double boiler over medium heat until milk is steaming but not boiling. Turn off the heat. Combine ¼ cup of the warm milk with the eggs yolks in a small bowl, stirring constantly. Add another ¼ cup of milk, stirring constantly to warm the egg yolks. Pour the egg-and-milk mixture back into the milk in the double boiler. Stir in the sugar. Turn on the heat to medium and cook, stirring constantly, until the mixture thickens slightly, about 10 minutes. The custard should be about the consistency of a creamy salad dressing and thickly coat the back of the wooden spoon.

When the custard mixture is thick, remove from the heat and put the top of the double boiler in the ice-water bath. Stir in the nutmeg. When the custard is cool, drizzle over individual servings of fruit salad and serve extra sauce on the side.

YIELD: 6 TO 8 SERVINGS
PREP TIME: 30 MINUTES
COOK TIME: 15 MINUTES

BREAKFAST BREAD PUDDING

Only make this bread pudding for people you really love, because they will want to be at your breakfast table every morning after they try this. I make it the night before and then pop it in the oven when I wake up. The smell drifts throughout the house and calls everyone to the kitchen.

1 tablespoon olive oil

1 medium yellow onion, minced

1 pound bulk breakfast sausage, crumbled

10 large eggs

3 cups milk

1 teaspoon kosher salt

½ teaspoon freshly ground black pepper

½ teaspoon garlic powder

1 loaf day-old brioche or country white bread, cut into 1½-inch cubes (about 12 cups)

2 cups shredded sharp Cheddar cheese (about 8 ounces)

Heat the olive oil in a medium skillet over medium heat. Add the onions and sauté until translucent, about 7 minutes. Add the sausage and brown, stirring to break up lumps, about 5 minutes. Using a slotted spoon, transfer to a shallow bowl and cool to room temperature.

In a large bowl, whisk the eggs, milk, salt, pepper, and garlic powder. Stir in the bread, sausage, and cheese. Butter a 13 by 9-inch baking dish, pour in the pudding, and cover with foil. Let the dish sit in the refrigerator for at least 1 hour and up to overnight.

Preheat the oven to 350° F.

Bake the pudding, still covered, for about 45 minutes. Remove the foil and bake 10 to 15 minutes more, until browned. Serve immediately.

YIELD: 6 TO 8 SERVINGS
PREP TIME: 20 MINUTES
INACTIVE PREP TIME: 1 HOUR TO OVERNIGHT
COOK TIME: 1 HOUR

DESSERTS

My grandmother had a T-shirt that said LIFE IS SHORT. EAT DESSERT FIRST. Words to live by, my friends. The most challenging part of baking a cake for me isn't the actual process; it's resisting the urge to cut into it before serving time.

A passion for sweet treats runs in my family. It's a competition of sorts. My great-grandmother, Pearl, won numerous blue ribbons for her angel food cakes. Her ambitions were passed down to my grandmother and her sister Pat, and their husbands self-servingly fanned the flames of their dessert-making rivalry. Lucky for me, I happily participated in the tasting and judging portion.

Desserts

GRANDMOTHER PAUL'S RED VELVET CAKE

COOKIES-AND-CREAM TRUFFLES

ROCKY ROAD FUDGE

CHOCOLATE PEANUT BUTTER CAKE

PEANUT BUTTER COOKIES

WEDDING BISCOTTI

BLACK FOREST TRIFLE

DARK CHOCOLATE CHUNK AND DRIED CHERRY COOKIES

CRANBERRY-PEAR CRISP

PEACH COBBLER

NO-BAKE CHOCOLATE OATMEAL COOKIE "COW PILES"

LEMON MERINGUE SQUARES

BANANA PUDDING PIE

STRAWBERRY SHORTCAKE

GRANDMOTHER PAUL'S RED VELVET CAKE

Recipe courtesy of Paula Deen

Paula Deen is a dear friend of mine and I love her grandmother's recipe for red velvet cake. The icing has the best texture from the cream cheese and marshmallow fluff combination, paired with the flaky coconut and crunchy pecans. In the South, it's common for red velvet cake to serve as the groom's cake at weddings. I like to make it for Valentine's Day.

For the cake

2 cups sugar

½ pound (2 sticks) butter, at room temperature

2 eggs

2 tablespoons cocoa powder

¼ cup red food coloring (two 1-ounce bottles)

2½ cups cake flour

1 teaspoon kosher salt

1 cup buttermilk

1 teaspoon pure vanilla extract

½ teaspoon baking soda

1 tablespoon distilled white vinegar

For the icing

One 8-ounce package cream cheese

8 tablespoons (1 stick) butter, softened

1 cup marshmallows, melted

One 1-pound package confectioners' sugar

1 cup shredded coconut

1 cup chopped pecans

FOR THE CAKE

Preheat the oven to 350° F. Grease and flour three 8-inch round cake pans.

In a large bowl, using a handheld electric mixer, cream the sugar and butter. Beat until light and fluffy. Add the eggs one at a time and mix well after each addition. In a small bowl, mix the cocoa and food coloring together. Add to the sugar mixture and mix well. Sift together the flour and salt. Add the flour mixture to the creamed mixture alternately with the buttermilk. Blend in the vanilla. In a small bowl, combine the baking soda and vinegar (it will foam) and stir into the batter. Pour the batter into the pans. Bake for 20 to 25 minutes, until a toothpick inserted into the center comes out clean. Remove from oven and cool completely on a wire rack before frosting.

FOR THE ICING

Beat the cream cheese and butter together in a medium bowl. Stir in the marshmallows and confectioners' sugar. Fold in the coconut and nuts. Spread between the layers and on the top and sides of cooled cake.

COOKIES-AND-CREAM TRUFFLES

One of my biggest weaknesses is a tall glass of milk and a package of Oreo cookies. I like to soak the cookies in the milk until they almost fall apart. These cookies-and-cream truffles are like bite-size Oreo cheesecakes. They can also be made with dark chocolate instead of white, and sometimes I coat half the batch in white chocolate and the other half in dark chocolate. If you use dark, dust with confectioners' sugar for contrast.

15 Oreo cookies

One 8-ounce package cream cheese

18 ounces white chocolate

1 to 2 tablespoons cocoa powder, for dusting

Line a baking sheet with parchment paper.

Place the cookies in a food processor and pulse until the cookies become fine crumbs. Add the cream cheese and pulse just until mixed. Using a melon baller or a teaspoon measure, scoop the cookie mixture into small balls. Place the cookie balls on the baking sheet. Cover the baking sheet with plastic and place in the freezer. Freeze the cookies until firm, about 1 hour.

Melt white chocolate in the top of a double boiler, or according to package instructions. Dip the cookie balls into the melted chocolate using a wooden skewer or fork and place back on the baking sheet. Place the cocoa powder in a fine-mesh sieve and dust the truffles lightly with cocoa. Cover the baking sheet with plastic and place back in the freezer. Freeze the truffles until firm, about 1 hour. Serve cold and store in the freezer.

YIELD: 50 TRUFFLES
PREP TIME: 1 HOUR
INACTIVE PREP TIME: 2 HOURS
COOK TIME: 15 MINUTES

PEANUT BUTTER COOKIES

Peanut butter cookies bring me right back to lunch in my elementary school cafeteria. The cooks would press each one with the back of a fork. I always tried to get an extra cookie, but those ladies were strict! Now I can have as many as my tummy desires.

1 cup all-purpose flour

½ teaspoon baking soda

¼ teaspoon kosher salt

8 tablespoons (1 stick) unsalted butter, room temperature

½ cup light brown sugar

½ cup granulated sugar

1 large egg

½ teaspoon pure vanilla extract

½ cup crunchy peanut butter

Preheat the oven to 325° F. Grease two cookie sheets.

In a small bowl, mix together the flour, baking soda, and salt.

In a medium bowl, use a handheld electric mixer to cream the butter and sugars until light and fluffy, about 4 minutes. Add the egg and beat until fully incorporated. Add the vanilla and the peanut butter and beat until fully incorporated. Add the flour mixture and beat until well mixed.

Using a tablespoon, drop the cookie dough onto the cookie sheets. Press each cookie lightly with a lightly floured fork. Bake for 15 to 18 minutes. Let cool on the baking sheets for 5 minutes and finish cooling on a wire rack.

YIELD: 32 COOKIES
PREP TIME: 15 MINUTES
COOK TIME: 20 MINUTES

WEDDING BISCOTTI

Rosemary is symbolic of remembrance. When I got married, I wanted to find a way to incorporate the herb into our special day. I came up with this recipe and sent each of our guests home with a tin packed with biscotti and included the recipe.

Preheat the oven to 350° F. Line a baking sheet with parchment paper.

In a small bowl, stir together the flour, baking powder, salt, and rosemary.

Using a handheld electric mixer, in a large mixing bowl beat the butter and sugar until light and fluffy, about 4 minutes. Add the eggs, one at a time, incorporating each egg fully before adding the next. Beat in the vanilla. Gently stir in the flour mixture until just combined. Stir in currants.

Cut dough in half and shape into two logs 12 inches long, 2½ inches wide, and 1 inch high. Bake until just starting to brown at the edges, about 35 minutes. Let cool for a few minutes on the baking sheets. Leave the oven turned on.

While the logs are still warm, cut each log into ½-inch-wide slices on the diagonal. Place the slices back on the baking sheet (use 2 baking sheets if necessary to fit all the slices). Bake for 7 to 8 minutes. Remove the baking sheets from the oven. Turn the biscotti over and bake for an additional 7 to 8 minutes, until the biscotti are crisp. Let the biscotti cool for a few minutes on the baking sheet(s). Serve when cooled to room temperature, or store in an airtight container for up to 2 weeks.

YIELD: 45 TO 50 BISCOTTI
PREP TIME: 20 MINUTES
COOK TIME: 45 MINUTES

- 3½ cups all-purpose flour
- 1 teaspoon baking powder
- ½ teaspoon kosher salt
- 2½ tablespoons finely chopped fresh rosemary
- 8 tablespoons (1 stick) unsalted butter, at room temperature
- ¾ cup sugar
- 3 eggs
- 1 teaspoon pure vanilla extract
- ¾ cup dried currants

BLACK FOREST TRIFLE

My grandmother's favorite cake is Black Forest, so I was thinking of her when I created this trifle. Unlike fussy desserts, trifles are actually supposed to be a little messy. It's also perfect for making ahead of time because the trifle is better after it has had some time for the layers to sink together.

For the cake

2 cups all-purpose flour

1½ cups sugar

½ cup cocoa powder

1½ teaspoons baking soda

¼ teaspoon baking powder

½ teaspoon kosher salt

½ cup canola oil

1 cup buttermilk

2 teaspoons pure vanilla extract

1 cup very hot strong coffee

For the chocolate pudding

1 cup sugar

½ cup all-purpose flour

1 cup cocoa powder

½ teaspoon kosher salt

1 quart reduced-fat milk

3 large egg yolks, lightly beaten

2 teaspoons pure vanilla extract

For the whipped cream

2 cups heavy whipping cream

½ cup sugar

1 teaspoon pure vanilla extract

For the trifle

Two 15-ounce cans pitted cherries, drained

FOR THE CAKE Preheat the oven to 350° F. Grease and flour a 13 by 9-inch baking pan. In a large bowl, sift together the flour, sugar, cocoa, baking soda, baking powder, and salt. Add the oil, buttermilk, and vanilla. Stir until just combined. Add the coffee and mix well. Pour into the pan and bake until a toothpick comes out clean, about 40 minutes. Cool the cake completely. Crumble the cake into medium chunks, cover, and set aside.

FOR THE CHOCOLATE PUDDING While the cake is baking, in a large saucepan over medium heat, combine the sugar, flour, cocoa, and salt, and mix well. Whisk in the milk. Stir constantly with a wooden spoon while the mixture comes up to a low boil and becomes thick, 7 to 9 minutes. Reduce the heat to very low. Stir a couple of tablespoons of the hot mixture into the egg yolks. Stir the egg yolks back into the hot mixture. Stir constantly until the mixture is thickened to the consistency of pudding, 3 to 4 minutes. Remove from the heat and stir in the vanilla. Cover with plastic wrap to prevent skin from forming and let cool.

FOR THE WHIPPED CREAM Using an electric mixer on high speed, beat the cream, sugar, and vanilla until stiff peaks form.

TO ASSEMBLE THE TRIFLE Put half of the cake crumbles in the bottom of a trifle dish. Top with half of the pudding. Layer with half of the cherries. Top with half the whipped cream. Repeat with remaining cake, pudding, cherries, and whipped cream. Save a few cherries or cake crumbs to garnish the top layer. Cover with plastic wrap and refrigerate for at least 2 hours, up to one day, until ready to serve.

YIELD: 6 TO 8 SERVINGS
PREP TIME: 20 MINUTES
INACTIVE PREP TIME: 2 HOURS TO 1 DAY
COOK TIME: 55 MINUTES

DARK CHOCOLATE CHUNK AND DRIED CHERRY COOKIES

I think of these as grown-up chocolate chip cookies. I love the intense, deep flavor of dark chocolate and the chewy, sweet dried cherries. Because there is a little less butter and sugar, the texture is much smoother and lighter than a typical chocolate chip cookie.

2 ¼ cups all-purpose flour

¾ teaspoon baking soda

1 teaspoon baking powder

1 teaspoon kosher salt

8 tablespoons (1 stick) unsalted butter, at room temperature

⅔ cup packed dark brown sugar

⅔ cup granulated sugar

2 large eggs

1 teaspoon pure vanilla extract

8 ounces dark chocolate, coarsely chopped

1 cup dried cherries (about 6 ounces), coarsely chopped

Preheat oven to 375° F. Position a rack in the middle of the oven. Grease two cookie sheets, or line with parchment paper.

In a medium bowl, sift together the flour, baking soda, baking powder, and salt.

In a large bowl, using a handheld electric mixer, cream the butter and sugars until light and fluffy, about 3 minutes. Add the eggs, one at a time beating until incorporated. Beat in the vanilla. Mix in the dry ingredients with the mixer on low speed until just combined. Stir in the chocolate and cherries with a wooden spoon.

Scoop by the heaping tablespoonful onto the cookie sheets. Bake until golden and chewy, 12 to 15 minutes. Transfer the cookies to a rack to cool. Store in an airtight container.

YIELD: 36 COOKIES
PREP TIME: 20 MINUTES
COOK TIME: 15 MINUTES

NO-BAKE CHOCOLATE OATMEAL COOKIE "COW PILES"

I used to beg my mom to make these cookies when I was a kid. Since they are so quick and easy, she usually would comply if I was behaving myself. You can use your imagination as to why I called them "cow piles."

2 cups sugar

8 tablespoons (1 stick) unsalted butter

⅓ cup cocoa powder

½ cup milk

1 teaspoon pure vanilla extract

½ cup peanut butter, creamy or crunchy

2½ to 3 cups rolled oats

In a medium saucepan, combine the sugar, butter, cocoa, milk, and vanilla. Bring to a slow boil and simmer until the sugar has dissolved. Stir in the peanut butter. Remove from the heat. Stir in 2½ cups oats. The mixture should be thick. Add the remaining ½ cup oats if necessary.

Line a cookie sheet with parchment paper. Drop the mixture by the heaping tablespoonful onto the parchment. Allow the cookies to firm up at room temperature, about 1 hour. Store in an airtight container.

YIELD: ABOUT 30 COOKIES
PREP TIME: 20 MINUTES
INACTIVE PREP TIME: 1 HOUR
COOK TIME: 5 MINUTES

LEMON MERINGUE SQUARES

Two of my grandfather's many favorite desserts were lemon squares and lemon meringue pie. I combined his favorites to make these lemon meringue squares. The walnuts add texture to the crust and pair nicely with the tart lemon.

Preheat the oven to 350° F. Butter an 8 by 8-inch baking dish.

In a large mixing bowl, cream the butter with ½ cup sugar until light and creamy. Add the egg yolks, one at a time. Add the lemon zest, salt, and vanilla and mix until combined. Slowly add the flour and ½ cup walnuts. Spread the mixture in the baking dish. Bake for 20 minutes. Remove from the oven, but leave the oven turned on.

Beat the egg whites and cream of tartar until stiff. Gradually beat in the remaining ½ cup sugar. Fold in the lemon juice and the remaining ½ cup walnuts. Spread over the hot baked layer. Bake for 25 minutes, until lightly browned. Cool completely before cutting.

YIELD: 4 TO 6 SERVINGS
PREP TIME: 15 MINUTES
COOK TIME: 45 MINUTES

8 tablespoons (1 stick) unsalted butter, softened

1 cup sugar

2 large eggs, separated

1 teaspoon grated lemon zest

¼ teaspoon kosher salt

½ teaspoon pure vanilla extract

1 cup all-purpose flour

1 cup coarsely chopped walnuts

¼ teaspoon cream of tartar

1 tablespoon fresh lemon juice

BANANA PUDDING PIE

Banana pudding is a staple on Southern dessert menus. I absolutely love the creamy vanilla pudding with the vanilla wafers and whipped cream. I got to thinking, what if I turned it into a pie? I crushed up the vanilla wafers and made the crust, lined it with bananas, filled it with pudding, and topped it with whipped cream. I ate the whole thing by myself!

For the pie

65 vanilla wafers (one box)

5⅓ tablespoons (⅔ stick) unsalted butter, melted

2 ripe medium bananas, thinly sliced

For the vanilla pudding

½ cup sugar

⅓ cup all-purpose flour

¼ teaspoon kosher salt

2 cups milk

4 large egg yolks, lightly beaten

2 teaspoons pure vanilla extract

For the whipped cream

1 cup heavy whipping cream

2 tablespoons sugar

1 teaspoon pure vanilla extract

YIELD: 6 TO 8 SERVINGS
PREP TIME: 40 MINUTES
INACTIVE PREP TIME: 3 HOURS
COOK TIME: 20 MINUTES

FOR THE PIE

Preheat the oven to 350° F. Grease a 9-inch pie plate.

FOR THE PUDDING

Place 45 vanilla wafers in a food processor and pulse the machine until the cookies are finely crushed. Reserve ¼ cup to top the pie. Mix the remaining crumbs with the melted butter. Firmly press into the pie plate to make a crust. Bake for 10 to 12 minutes. Remove from the oven and cool.

Meanwhile, make the vanilla pudding: In a medium saucepan over medium heat, combine the sugar, flour, and salt. Whisk in the milk and stir constantly with a wooden spoon until the mixture comes to a low boil and becomes thick, about 7 minutes. Reduce the heat to very low. Stir a couple of tablespoons of the hot milk mixture into the egg yolks. Stir the egg yolks back into the hot mixture. Stir constantly until the mixture is thickened to the consistency of pudding, 3 to 4 minutes. Remove from heat and stir in the vanilla.

Arrange half of the banana slices over the crust. Spread about half of the pudding over the bananas, top with the remaining 20 vanilla wafers. Top the wafers with the remaining bananas and pudding. Let cool completely.

FOR THE WHIPPED CREAM

Using an electric mixer, beat the cream, sugar, and vanilla until soft peaks form.

Spread the whipped cream over the pie and sprinkle with the reserved crumbs. Cover with plastic wrap and refrigerate up to one day, until serving.

STRAWBERRY SHORTCAKE

When I was a little girl, my grandmother planted a strawberry patch with me. I would rush out every morning to "monitor" the berries' progress, stealing a couple each time; with my ruby-stained fingers I fooled no one. Unlike the oversized strawberries with hard, white centers we buy at the supermarket, those homegrown berries were petite and juicy. My grandmother would make the most incredible strawberry shortcake. The cake is more of a giant sweet biscuit than a cake, and she always doubled the recipe for the strawberries because she knew that I would take an extra serving.

FOR THE STRAWBERRIES

In a medium bowl, mix the strawberries and sugar. Set aside, covered, for at least 30 minutes and up to 3 hours in order for the sugar and strawberries to make a sauce. The longer this sits, the juicier the strawberries will become.

FOR THE CAKE

Preheat the oven to 450° F. Grease an 8-inch round cake pan.

In a large bowl, mix the flour, sugar, baking powder, and salt. Using a pastry blender, cut in the butter until it makes a fine meal. Make a well in the center, and stir in milk and buttermilk until blended. (It will have a biscuit dough–like consistency.) Spoon into the cake pan. Use floured hands to pat the mixture into the pan. Bake until golden brown on top and a toothpick comes out clean, 15 to 20 minutes. Remove from the oven and cool slightly.

While the cake is still warm, split it in half horizontally to make two thin layers. Remove the top layer and spoon the berries and their juices onto the bottom layer of the cake. Replace the top layer.

Serve with whipped cream or
vanilla ice cream.

For the strawberries

1 quart strawberries, stemmed and sliced in half

1 cup sugar

For the cake

2 cups all-purpose flour

2 tablespoons sugar

3 teaspoons baking powder

1 teaspoon kosher salt

8 tablespoons (1 stick) unsalted butter, chilled and cut into cubes

¾ cup milk

½ cup buttermilk

YIELD: 6 TO 8 SERVINGS
PREP TIME: 10 MINUTES
INACTIVE PREP TIME: 30 MINUTES TO 3 HOURS
COOK TIME: 20 MINUTES

DRINKS

When I entertain, I make a signature cocktail for each party. I usually make a pitcher in advance and set up a bar area, complete with glasses, stirrers, and cocktail napkins, in the room where I'm serving hors d'oeuvres. I like to make a nonalcoholic option, as well. Guests can then help themselves.

Drinks

ICED SWEET TEA

KIR ROYALE

LEMONADE

BOURBON SLUSH

ANNE'S SPICED COFFEE

PEACH FIZZ

POLAR BEAR

AHMAD'S MARGA-TINI

WHITE COSMOPOLITAN

ICED SWEET TEA

If there were an official beverage of the South, it would be sweet tea. I only call for a half-cup sugar, but adjust it to your taste. I have friends who put in a whole cup, some even a cup and a half!

4 tea bags, such as Lipton or Luzianne

½ cup sugar

4 cups boiling water

Place the tea bags and sugar in a heatproof pitcher. Pour the boiling water over and let the tea steep about 5 minutes. Remove the tea bags and stir until the sugar is dissolved. Cool to room temperature and serve over ice.

Garnish with mint or lemon slices.

YIELD: 4 CUPS (4 TO 6 SERVINGS)
PREP TIME: 5 MINUTES
INACTIVE PREP TIME: 1 HOUR

KIR ROYALE

When I travel to Paris, I love staying at the George V. The hotel has the most beautiful bar in the lobby, and I go every night before dinner for an aperitif. I always order a Kir royale (Champagne with a touch of cassis). When I'm home, longing for Paris, I make this chic cocktail.

Crème de cassis

Chilled Champagne

Pour ½ teaspoon cassis into each Champagne glass. Fill with Champagne and serve immediately.

YIELD: 1 DRINK
PREP TIME: 5 MINUTES

LEMONADE

I love a refreshing glass of lemonade on a hot summer day. Juicing lemons by hand is exhausting and frustrating, so I recommend using an electric citrus juicer. You will be surprised how much you use it, not only for making lemonade or orange juice, but also when cooking recipes that call for fresh lemon or lime juice. Try mixing equal parts lemonade and sweet tea for a drink called an "Arnold Palmer."

Combine the ingredients in a large pitcher. Stir until the sugar dissolves completely. Chill until serving time or serve immediately over ice.

YIELD: 6 TO 8 SERVINGS
PREP TIME: 10 MINUTES

1 cup fresh lemon juice (about 5 lemons)

4 cups cold water

½ cup superfine sugar

1 cup ice

BOURBON SLUSH

In Huntington, West Virginia, Kay Earles is a hometown regular at every Marshall University football game. She is famous for her bourbon slushes and always shows up before games with plenty to go around. It's very easy to spot her car in the packed tailgating lot because of the massive crowd of thirsty people clamoring for one of her slushes.

3 cups bourbon

24 ounces frozen lemonade concentrate, thawed

12 ounces frozen orange juice concentrate, thawed

4 cups strong brewed tea

In a very large pitcher or bowl (at least 1½ gallons capacity), mix together the bourbon, frozen concentrates, and tea. Stir to mix. Stir in 3 quarts water. Place in the freezer. Stir after 8 hours. Continue to freeze for 2 hours more, and up to 2 days. Take out of the freezer 30 minutes before serving. Stir and serve.

YIELD: 8 TO 10 SERVINGS
PREP TIME: 5 MINUTES
INACTIVE PREP TIME: 9 HOURS

ANNE'S SPICED COFFEE

My dear friend Anne is known for her coffee. She is the perfect houseguest because she gets up early and puts a pot on, filling the house with its spicy aroma. I especially like it during the holiday season and winter months.

Fill the filter of a coffee maker with the ground coffee beans, cinnamon, cloves, and orange zest. Fill the coffee maker with water to make 8 cups coffee and brew.

Serve hot.

8 scoops coffee (8 tablespoons)

2 teaspoons ground cinnamon

1 teaspoon whole cloves

Zest of 1 orange

YIELD: 4 SERVINGS
PREP TIME: 5 MINUTES
COOK TIME: 10 MINUTES

PEACH FIZZ

When peaches are in season, I eat them every day. I usually just cut them up on my cereal or make a peach cobbler, but when I'm feeling especially festive, I make this peach fizz.

6 fresh peaches (about 2 pounds), peeled and roughly chopped (about 5 cups)

One 6-ounce can frozen lemonade concentrate

¼ cup gin

½ cup ice

Fresh mint sprigs

Combine peaches, lemonade, gin, and ice in a blender. Make in batches if necessary. Blend until smooth. Pour into cocktail glasses and garnish with mint sprigs.

YIELD: ABOUT 5½ CUPS (4 SERVINGS)
PREP TIME: 8 MINUTES

POLAR BEAR

This is like a grown-up coffee milkshake. I love the flavor of the vanilla ice cream mixed with the coffee liqueur. It will cool you down in the summer and warm you up in the winter!

Put four dessert glasses in the freezer.

Whip the cream with the sugar until soft peaks form.

Combine ice cream, milk, and coffee liqueur in a blender. Blend until smooth. Serve in the dessert glasses, topped with a dollop of whipped cream and a sprinkle of cocoa.

YIELD: 4 SERVINGS
PREP TIME: 5 TO 7 MINUTES

½ cup heavy whipping cream

1 tablespoon confectioners' sugar

1 pint vanilla ice cream

1½ cups milk

½ cup coffee-flavored liqueur

Cocoa powder

AHMAD'S MARGA-TINI

I love a margarita just as much as the next girl, but so often bartenders make them overly sweet, or just use a mix. After drinking one, I end up feeling like I don't even want my dinner. My friend Ahmad makes this drink that I've coined the marga-tini because it's not quite a margarita, but more like a martini made with tequila. It is so light and refreshing.

Fill a cocktail shaker with ice. Add the tequila, lime juice, and Rose's lime juice. Shake until mixed and chilled, about 30 seconds. Strain over ice in a cocktail glass and top with the club soda. Garnish with a lime wedge.

YIELD: 1 SERVING
PREP TIME: 5 MINUTES

Crushed ice

⅓ cup white tequila

1 tablespoon fresh lime juice

2 tablespoons Rose's lime juice

¼ cup club soda or seltzer

Lime wedge

WHITE COSMOPOLITAN

I love cosmopolitans. Only problem is, the cranberry juice leaves a serious stain if you spill one. These are made with white cranberry juice, so they are perfect for a party.

1 cup citron-flavored vodka

½ cup Cointreau

½ cup white cranberry juice

¼ cup fresh lime juice

Ice cubes

Combine the vodka, Cointreau, cranberry juice, and lime juice in a large cocktail shaker filled with ice. Shake for about 15 seconds and strain into martini glasses.

YIELD: 4 DRINKS
PREP TIME: 5 MINUTES

ACKNOWLEDGMENTS

Writing this book truly has been one of the greatest experiences of my life. I enjoyed every minute of it, from writing the outline and developing the recipes to the photo shoot; I even enjoyed the editing process. For a project of this kind, a successful collaboration is key, and getting there isn't always a smooth process. Luckily for me, I was fortunate enough to have a team of wonderful, easygoing people who made work a pleasure, and to have my family and friends, who provided amazing support.

I offer tremendous thanks and gratitude to Bill, my husband. He was the best little guinea pig . . . always honest. He makes me a stronger person. My family—Mom, Dad, Jim, Grandma, Pat, Grandma Bonnie . . . all of you—I love you with all my heart. Oh, how I wish both Grandpa and Larry could see all of this and join us one more time at the dinner table.

At S&S, thank you to Jen Bergstrom, my publisher, for believing in me and for her enthusiasm. Tricia Boczkowski, my editor, for painstakingly editing and for pushing me to do my best. Michael Nagin put together an excellent cover, and Jane Archer did an unbelievable job with the design.

Miki Duisterhof, my photographer, and her assistants, Barbara Naegle and Colleen MacMillen, were delightful to work with and so talented. Paul Lowe and his assistants, Matthew Burdi and Abbey Cook, did a beautiful job with the food and prop styling. It is very rare to work on a photo shoot for two weeks with a group of people and actually *miss* them when it is over. Thanks to the folks at Sant Ambroeus, Citarella, Pike's Farm Stand, and The Seafood Shop in Wainscott for letting us photograph there.

I thank Katrina Norwood, who thoroughly tested each recipe for accuracy and was a pleasure to work with, even though we were across the country from each other (thank goodness for technology!).

Thanks to Ahmad Sardar-Afkhami and Nate Berkus, both great friends, who designed a fabulous kitchen for me, in which I was able to create all of these recipes and use as my photo studio.

Very special thanks to Yigal Azrouel, my friend and favorite designer, for continuing to create brilliant collections and for designing my wardrobe for this book. Donata Minelli, Johnna Campbell, and Katie Fassler facilitated all of my clothing requests at a moment's notice. Also, thanks to my "glam squad," Marc Mena and Julie Tussey.

On the business side, thanks to Andy McNichol, my literary agent, and to Jon Rosen, Jason Hodes, and Andrew Muser for keeping me employed. Thanks to my lawyer, Lee Eastman, and my business manager, Todd Kamelhar, for the best advice. Thanks to my publicist, Rebecca Brooks, for so many great ideas. Extra big, big thanks to my assistant, Keri Aylward; without her, I really could not function.

A big heartfelt thanks to my fairy godmother, Paula Deen, and her husband, Michael. In the few years we have known each other, I have come to feel like they are part of my extended family. Love to y'all . . . and Brandon and Corrie, too.

I am genuinely blessed to have the most fantastic friends a girl could ever ask for: Kelli Morgan, Anne Thornton, Marcy Blum, Gretchen Monahan, Stephanie Jones, Wendi Murdoch, Ellen Cyrus, Beth Ostrosky, Alicia Ghiz, Biana Stepanian, Michael Schlow, and Lee Schrager. And thanks to my friend Giada de Laurentiis, who guided and advised me throughout the process of writing this book. Without all of them, life just wouldn't be as fun!

Thank you, thank you . . . from the bottom of my heart.

APPENDIX

MEASURING EQUIVALENTS

1 tablespoon = 3 teaspoons

⅛ cup = 2 tablespoons

¼ cup = 4 tablespoons

⅓ cup = 5 tablespoons + 1 teaspoon

½ cup = 8 tablespoons

⅔ cup = 10 tablespoons + 2 teaspoons

¾ cup = 12 tablespoons

1 cup = 16 tablespoons

8 fluid ounces = 1 cup

1 pint = 2 cups

1 quart = 2 pints

4 cups = 1 quart

1 gallon = 4 quarts

16 ounces = 1 pound

BAKING PAN SUBSTITUTIONS

10 by 2-inch round = 9 by 9 by 2-inch square

12 cup muffin tin = 8½ by 4½ by 2½-inch loaf

9 by 2-inch round = two 8 by 1½-inch rounds = 8 by 8 by 2-inch square

*NOTE: *Baking times vary depending on the pan size.*

CUTLERY

A cook's knife is an extension of his or her hand. Invest in a high-quality chef's knife, like a Wüsthof or a Global. Hold it in the store and make sure that the handle feels good in your hand and that the weight of the knife feels balanced. Don't waste your money on an expensive knife set. There are only three knives that are essential for every kitchen: an 8-inch chef's knife, a paring knife, and a serrated bread knife.

Always, *always* be sure to have a sharp knife. Not only is it much safer, but it is much more efficient. If you are not comfortable sharpening your knives at home with a whetstone, take them to a store that sells cutlery or ask your butcher to sharpen them. Don't put your knives in the dishwasher or leave them soaking in water for long periods of time.

POTS AND PANS

When it comes to my cookware, I go for the quality goods. Pots and pans are items that are okay to splurge on—when properly cared for, the good ones last a lifetime. I use mostly Le Creuset and All-Clad. Both are heavy duty and can be used on the stove and in the oven.

I also love my old-fashioned cast-iron skillet, which is a great conductor of heat. I use mine on the stove top but also for baking cornbread. A good cast-iron skillet must be properly seasoned. Many stores sell seasoned skillets, but you can do it at home by coating the pan with a vegetable oil and placing it in a 300° F oven for one hour. Remove the pan from the oven and let it cool to room temperature. Then wipe out the remaining oil and store. Once a pan is properly seasoned, it should be fairly nonstick. I season mine once every few months. To clean cast iron, do not use soap and water, just rub it clean with a dishcloth. Never put your cast-iron skillet in the dishwasher or let it soak in water, because it will rust.

KITCHEN GADGETS AND TOOLS

Here is a list of the equipment you will need in order to have a well-stocked kitchen:

- Cutting boards: one plastic for meats and one wooden for everything else
- Measuring cups and spoons
- Rubber spatulas
- Flat spatulas
- Pastry brushes
- Tongs
- Box grater and microplane grater
- Zester
- Wooden spoons
- Whisks
- Food processor
- Blender
- Immersion blender
- Electric mixer (handheld and/or standing)
- Pizza cutter
- Panini grill
- Citrus juicer
- Coffee grinder (I have two, one for coffee, one for spices)
- Slow cooker
- Nonstick baking mat

INDEX